pure

The Spirituality of Desire

sex

Other books by Gordon Dalbey

Healing the Masculine Soul

Sons of the Father
Healing the Father-Wound in Men Today

Fight like a Man
A New Manhood for a New Warfare

No Small Snakes
A Journey into Spiritual Warfare

Broken by Religion, Healed by God
*Restoring the Evangelical, Sacramental,
Pentecostal, Social Justice Church*

Do Pirates Wear Pajamas?
and Other Mysteries in the Adventure of Fathering

Religion vs. Reality
Facing the Home Front in Spiritual Warfare

Loving to Fight or Fighting to Love?
Winning the Spiritual Battle for Your Marriage

Gordon Dalbey may be reached
for resources and speaking engagements at
www.abbafather.com
Box 61042, Santa Barbara, CA 93160

pure

The Spirituality of Desire

sex

GORDON DALBEY

with

MARY ANDREWS-DALBEY, PhD

CivitasPress

Publishing inspiring and redemptive ideas.℠

Pure Sex, The Spirituality of Desire

with a chapter by Mary Andrews-Dalbey, PhD

ISBN #978-0692344743

Published by Civitas Press, LLC

San Jose, CA

www.civitaspress.com

Contents

It's not that we lack the discipline to repress sexual desire,
but rather, the faith to embrace it as God intends.

Sexual desire is a holy nostalgia for Paradise.

There's no such thing as a "sexual need."
Nobody ever died from lack of sex.

Religion reduces desire to manageable morality,
divorcing it from spirituality and infecting it with shame.

The human body is the temple of the Spirit;
the woman's womb is the Holy of holies.

Couples argue to determine, Who's right?
The real question is, What's God trying to teach us?

Sex without a commitment
destroys a woman's heart.

Shame-less tolerance
has supplanted shame-ful morality.

The impulse to modesty cannot be overridden
without beckoning the shame of our sin-nature.

Femininity blossoms amid security;
masculinity thrives amid insecurity.

Sexual freedom is not the absence of restriction,
but the presence of the Father, who enables its created purpose.

Loneliness is the natural human state of aloneness
when not surrendered to God.

Insofar as the woman bears grace,
religion fears femininity.

Love is not a goal to be achieved,
but a blessing to be received.

It's not about making your marriage work,
but about letting God work in your marriage.

There's more to sex than mere skin on skin. Sex
is as much spiritual mystery as physical fact.
(1 Corinth. 6:16,17TMB)

> **Humbled and amazed, I receive this powerful mystery with all its promise and warning.**

Foreword

So God created man in his own image, in the image of God he created him; male and female he created them.
Genesis 1:27 NIV

WHEN I FIRST BEGAN TELLING OTHERS about this book, many were startled by the title. "I've never heard the words 'sex' and 'spirituality' in the same sentence!" as one declared. "When you hear the word 'spirituality' you think of church. But church is the last place you'd expect to hear someone talking about sex."

That's sad. Worse, it's dangerous. Banning sexuality from church leaves a vacuum which the world is literally hell-bent to fill. "Sex is dirty and immoral," as the culture confounds, "so save it for marriage and the one you love most!"

Yet if God created sex as a reflection of His very image in male and female together, it must be good. Marriage, therefore, does not make sex good anymore than a fireplace makes a fire hot. Rather, the covenant with God contains and focuses desire so it can safely accomplish His good purposes–including the pleasure of His son and daughter together.

When my son reached puberty, I told him that the power of sexual desire is like a fire burning in your body. God has designed a place for that fire to burn, I explained--like the living room fireplace he enjoyed so much as a boy. If you keep the blaze in the fireplace, it warms the home so everyone draws closer—even to have fun together roasting marshmallows and popcorn. But if you light the fire outside the fireplace, it'll burn the house down.

God's sexual boundaries are not a slave master's commands to deprive us of pleasure, but rather, a Father's invitation to enjoy each other safely under His covering. Even as a magnifying glass focuses a sunbeam, that is, the marriage covenant intensifies desire.

Since the Fall at Creation, however, human nature draws us to miss the mark of God's calling. This inborn impulse to sin leaves us all with an abiding shame. That's why Jesus came: to bear that shame on the cross, redeem our sin-nature with the Father's grace, free us to receive His Spirit, and thereby empower us to fulfill His calling.

In our natural ability, that is, we can't measure up to our created purpose. The human cry to overcome that deep and crippling shame draws the heart of Father God like none other to save His children. At the same time, by virtue of its organic intensity and universal longing for release, that cry draws the enemy of God as blood draws a shark.

My previous books about wounding in men, division among churches, and the denial of spiritual warfare have revealed shame as the root instigator of 'all the above'. To see that same culprit behind the widespread misconception of sexuality today, we need only look in a mirror.

Certainly, any credible presentation on sexuality requires both male and female input. I write here out of my own perspective as a man. I'm pleased, therefore, to include a chapter "Sexual Bonding and a Woman's Heart" by my wife Mary, a psychologist who ministers widely to women—and who witnesses eminently to the feminine perspective. Indeed, her wisdom and grace pervade my stories here.

At the very genesis of creation, in fact, Adam and Eve's fig leaves testified that sexuality bears the primary burden of our shame from Original Sin. Any open and faithful discussion about sexuality therefore requires facing down the primal roots of shame and disowning its condemnation.

That's precisely what Jesus empowered us to do. "God gave the Law through Moses, but grace and truth came through Jesus Christ," as John proclaimed (John 1:17). "Therefore," Paul concludes, "there is now no condemnation for those who are in Christ Jesus" (Rom. 8:1).

Needless to say, the world has not fully embraced Jesus and these boons of His ministry. Both our sin-nature and spiritual powers opposed to God yet conspire to sabotage His saving work among us—via outright destruction or more subtle counterfeits. Among the latter, as we'll see, no false shame-remover preys upon our sin-nature and distorts sexuality so seductively as religion.

The eternal question therefore remains: "Will the Son of Man find faith on earth when He comes?" (Luke 18:8). Certainly, He'll find religion aplenty, that is, people striving to prove they're good—or at least, better than you—instead of confessing they can't be good and crying out for a savior (see Rom. 7:18-8:1).

HIDDEN IN PLAIN VIEW

Credible faith, meanwhile, is not about either fantasy or dogma, but rather, an awareness of God at work in this world. It's simple, but not easy. Often, in fact, the most pervasive aspects of life are so commonly assumed that we hardly notice them. Even as sexuality infuses creation itself, therefore, its impact can be hidden in plain view.

It's astonishing when you think about it. The image of the Creator God is reflected in the union of man and woman. Manifested sexually, that union creates new life. In fact, all mammals and most other animals—from elephants to spiders—are created either male or female. In each species, the draw to unite is necessary to perpetuate its kind.

Where does that universal, life-defining power originate? Among human beings, does it serve any purpose beyond procreation? If so, how can we cooperate with God and each other to fulfill it?

Even as a long journey begins with a single step, the search after answers for such far-reaching questions often begins amid everyday experience. Like the proverbial drop of pond water under a microscope, a simple day's chronicle can reveal wonders to those with eyes to see.

Walking down the main street of our town, for example, amid the crowds I notice two distinct kinds of people: male and female. Looking for a public rest room, I find two separate doors, marked "Men" and "Women."

At my local discount store haunt, women's clothes occupy the first floor, while men's wear hides downstairs in one, notably smaller section.

Men's shoe options are limited to two small counters, about a dozen pairs; women's shoes occupy almost half the first floor. "It's more fun to be a woman," Mary laughs. "You get to express yourself differently every day!"

Further down the street, the old joke holds:

What do you call the women's section of a bookstore?

The bookstore.

Searching for a birthday card for my sister, I visit several drugstores. Amid many generic "To My Sister" and more specific sister-to-sister options—plus one or two from sister to brother—there are no Happy Birthday cards explicitly from brother to sister.

Back home, I add my son to the family auto insurance policy and note that the cost for female drivers his age is less than the cost for young men, who statistically cause more accidents.

GENDER BALANCE

In family conversation, I refer to our cat as "she." That's because we have only one child, a son. When we began looking for a pet cat years ago, Mary declared—not entirely in jest—that she was glad we found a female kitten to "gender balance" our family.

We all laughed. One morning as Mary was putting on makeup, however, even she was taken aback when Coco leapt up onto the vanity table alongside and began licking her paw and washing her face! Coco does not join me shaving in my bathroom.

Not having a daughter, I'm aware that when our son brings his girlfriend over, the gender balance is decisively restored to our home. At mealtime, the atmosphere around the table, once weighted by two hungry men, seems brighter and more engaging. Dinner conversation once dominated by weightlifting techniques and shark attacks now includes the best place to get your nails done and what spices made the sauce so tasty. Timely topics from global warming to terrorism, gun control, and feminism stir lively debates among the four of us.

I'm reminded of a proverb among the Igbo people, with whom I lived years ago in rural Nigeria as a Peace Corps Volunteer: "A house without a daughter is like a house without a window."

In the newspaper, a female candidate is touted as possibly the first woman President of the United States. Amid the political buzz, I marvel that my grandmother, born in 1891, was not allowed to vote until she was almost thirty years old.

An opinion editorial charges that male workers still rise up the company ladder faster and better paid than equally qualified women. News stories reflect that male politicians, entertainers, clergy, military leaders, athletes, and other prominent figures fall in disgrace to illicit sexual activity more often than their female counterparts.

Later on TV, it's clear that the popular music and sit-com industries thrive on romantic boy-meets-girl themes about love lost, gained, or anticipated. At the same time, same-sex attraction is a featured issue from legislature to pulpit.

Meanwhile, workers protest for minimum wage while a woman gets paid thousands of dollars for simply taking off her clothes in front of a camera. My men's conferences rarely draw as many as a hundred; another news item notes a woman who appeared in Times Square in naught but see-through lingerie and drew an immediate audience of thousands, plus far more via media coverage.[1]

Don't get me wrong. I'm not jealous. Just under-exposed.

I'm sure you can add your own observations to this ever-expanding list. On and on, the vast impact of sexuality generates life, upends history, shapes the culture, beckons the future—and boggles the mind.

Amazingly, however, its organic roots and ordained focus remain obscured in a world utterly blinded by natural reality.

Humbled and awed, I receive this powerful mystery with all its warning and promise.

Like all mysteries, sexual desire stirs with both fear and excitement. As one writer notes amid today's heated debate at colleges over what constitutes sexual consent, "The reality is that much of sex is not consensual—but it is also not non-consensual. It resides in a gray area in between, where sexual experimentation and discovery happen. Sex is inherently dangerous…. Trying to shoehorn sex into a strict yes-or-no consent framework in an attempt to make it risk-free can't help but destroy it."[2]

The fear of sexual desire, that is, stems from not being able to control the outcome, which might upend our truncated but otherwise comfortable worldview.

Likewise, the excitement.

```
┌─────────────────────────────────────────┐
│              CAUTION !                    │
│  You are about to enter the spirit realm. │
│  Powers you will engage after this point are │
│  beyond your ability to control.          │
└─────────────────────────────────────────┘
```

Introduction

Embracing the Mystery

There are four things that are too mysterious for me to
understand:
an eagle flying in the sky,
a snake moving on a rock,
a ship finding its way over the sea,
and a man and a woman falling in love.
Prov. 30:18,19

IF YOU'RE HOLDING THIS BOOK or digital device in your hands right now, that's a physical act. Your fingers touch it, triggering a sensation through your nerves that registers in your brain. It's a bodily phenomenon, a biologically certified fact. Beyond the intricacy of the human body's communication system, we're not moved to marvel.

Just seeing someone of the opposite sex across the room, however, can stir a dynamic response. Eyes move, pulse rates jump, and bodies are literally drawn toward each other.

Clear physical impact without physical connection.

How does that happen?

"Animal magnetism," the world offers—in an attempt to cover the shame of our unknowing by reducing the power to a manageable category. Animals, that is, can be controlled with cages and guns, and magnetic force fields can be explained by the physics of sub-atomic particle charges.

Certainly, natural willpower may "cage" sexual response and the crippling firepower of shame may punish its abuse. Neither tactic, however, can eliminate the impulse that draws a man and woman together.

Similarly, governments invested billions of dollars in particle physics to track down the vaunted Higgs-Boson "God particle," hailed as the basic building block of the universe. But no scientist has yet discovered any atomic forces—sub or otherwise—driving sexual attraction. Wisely, nations budget no money to research the physics of sexual desire, even as that energy literally infuses the very roots of creation.

SEX HAPPENS

To complicate matters for our Western scientific mindset, there's no wire between his belly button and hers—not even a microchip or any remote control mechanism to transmit and receive data. Nevertheless—flying in the face of our otherwise rationally ordered world—sexual attraction happens, with all its upending power, pleasure, fear, and as the Bible notes, mystery.

Unlike us, the ancient Hebrews who embraced the opening Proverbs confession were not so overly educated in manageable fact, nor enamored thereby of their own natural abilities, as to obscure larger, *super*-natural reality. Proverbs, in fact, is a letter of life instruction from a father to his son (see Prov. 1:8). Openly, humbly—albeit shamefully to our Western conceit—he confesses that there are things in this world "too mysterious for me to understand."

I like this dad. He's both truthful and gracious in telling his son it's OK not to know everything. In fact, he seizes the "birds and bees" occasion—from which we modern dads often cower—and redeems it boldly to deliver his son from the shame of unknowing.

Still, we must of course understand that these primitive biblical folk lacked our own great knowledge and sophisticated worldview today.

"An eagle flying in the sky"? Obviously, the writer never studied simple aerodynamics, how the bird's wing is curved just so air moving across the top lowers the pressure above with respect to that below, which lifts it up.

"A snake moving on a rock"? Even in my 1950s high school biology class we learned that a snake's muscles configure not lengthwise, but rather, as a spiral and thereby squeeze it along as a spring or "slinky" toy.

"A ship finding its way over the sea"? GPS and radar—done.

But hold on.

Amid our otherwise comforting hubris, one great mystery in this list remains. So great, in fact, that it not only trumps the others, but confounds science and all natural forms of knowing. Last, but manifestly not least on his list of phenomena "too mysterious" to understand, this father notes, "A man and a woman falling in love"—that is, "The way of a man with a maiden" (NIV).

HOLY DYNAMICS

Sexual attraction is the issue here, as the consummate challenge to our rational understanding. It's the Mystery of mysteries, in fact—so common and yet so powerful, so integral to creation itself as to trump all human knowledge and wisdom. And so this ancient Bible sage warns us modern self-satisfied fools: No matter how intelligent and scientifically accomplished you may be—how much aerodynamics, biology, or physics you master—you'll never be able fully to control nor understand the holy dynamics of sexuality.

If that's your goal here, you're holding the wrong book. Better you should be reading a fairy tale or appliance manual.

The pathway to truth is paved with humility. If you're ready to confess that sexual desire is ultimately beyond your natural ability to control—even as it both threatens and promises to be so—welcome to reality.

Read on.

Sexual desire, in fact, is a spiritual phenomenon. As such, it originates not in our bodies but in the spirit realm.

Among people who acknowledge and respect spiritual power, this revelation prompts awe, even worship—as, for example, in Old Testament Canaan and New Testament Corinth. In today's secularized Western culture, however, sexual desire prompts fear and shame, because we can't control it.

We might say that your body, like a TV, transforms the sexual broadcast signal from an external, spiritual source into a physical/bodily manifestation. But the quality of the TV receiver determines the quality of the reception. God's pure intention for sex, that is, does not often manifest purely in us sin-infected, spiritually challenged human beings. As in all aspects of life, the divine Word on sexual desire loses something in the worldly translation—something essential, in fact, to its origin and fulfillment.

For better or worse, sexual attraction stirs independently from human will. Its purpose, therefore, cannot be fulfilled apart from the God who created it.

Lacking spiritual sensitivity yet engaged by sexual power, our "modern" culture is at best confused and at worst, frightened. Diligently, we delude ourselves by reducing desire to a physical, even marketable commodity—as with alluring commercial models, pharmaceutical props like Viagra, and pornographic media. Ultimately, however, we tacitly acknowledge the spiritual nature of sexuality by worshipping—that is, attributing vitality and saving power to—the celebrity hunk or sex goddess who can conjure the most powerful spirit of lust.

It may be helpful to note here that "the enemy" and particular "spirits" refer to negative spiritual entities reported in the Bible, whose goal unto today is to distort the image of Father God and sabotage His purposes among us. Since God's image is most explicitly reflected in the union of male and female, the enemy's most fierce efforts to discredit God focus deliberately, even primarily, on misrepresenting sexuality. The term "deliverance" refers to the process of being set free from those forces.

If this dark dimension of spirituality is hard to accept, I understand all too well. In fact, my book *No Small Snakes: A Journey into Spiritual Warfare* tells how my rational skepticism was decisively upended by experiences which forced me to face it.

In any case, at our genesis, God declared humanity and sexuality "very good" along with the rest of creation (Gen. 1:31NIV). As a loving Father, however, He gave us free will to receive or reject Him—an exceedingly risky venture, as the vast brokenness in the world testifies. What's more, in addition to our natural human propensity to turn away from God, destructive spiritual powers are at work in this world to turn us against Him.

Years ago as a high school freshman, I learned this simple but elusive truth—not, I'm obliged to note, in any officially ordained classroom.

GATHERED FERVENTLY

One afternoon when classes finished early for a teachers' meeting, I dashed out to my school bus anxious to seize a front row seat. Passing through the doors, I ascended the staircase and entered this holy chamber. Thankfully, I beheld the empty seats—except for the back row, in which several of my classmates were gathered fervently around some old guy in a dark Levi jacket.

He must have been at least seventeen.

Curious, I dropped my books on a front row seat and walked inquisitively down the aisle back toward my friends. After a few steps, I slowed as an undefined yet palpable energy hovered strangely in the air.

"Hi,…guys," I offered tentatively. "What's…"

"Shh!" one burst out with a loud whisper, his gaze fixed with the others upon the elder in denim garb. "Shut up and sit down!"

At once, it occurred to me that these friends never told me to shut up and sit down in math class—where the teacher had to shout and threaten us with an office visit to make us pay attention.

Puzzled, yet duly respectful, I eased reverently into a nearby pew.

With a sharp glance in my direction, our senior evangelist for puberty continued his sermon, soon citing something he'd done with his girlfriend in the back seat of his car the night before. As all freshman eyes fixed upon him, he paused.

Seizing the opportunity, one of my friends raised his hand—a gesture of respect rarely extended to the math teacher.

"Yeah, kid?" the elder acknowledged sternly. "Waddaya want?"

"I wonder…," the novitiate managed, intimidated yet determined. "I mean…"

"Speak up, kid! Waddizzit?"

"Well, how…, I mean, how will I know when…when I wanna do that?"

TON OF BRICKS

Snickering and sweeping his tender congregation with a sneer, this man of the denim cloth leaned forward righteously with a sharp benediction. "Kid," he shot back, "it's gonna hit you like a tonna *bricks!*"

Startled, I drew up along with my fellow disciples. As other students began entering the bus, without further ado we each split hurriedly for a window seat and a long, long ride home—with the words "ton of bricks" resounding in our bodies.

I had attended church throughout my youth, yet never had I been so seized by a Sunday school lesson or sermon. Yes, I'd been taught that God is the Creator of all things. *But could that possibly include sex?*

Some weeks later, in the midst of algebra class, I understood—or at least, attested.

Taking notes as the teacher spoke, I was jarred by a loud THWOCK! as a book hit the floor behind me. Turning to look, I saw one of my skirted female classmates two rows away bend over, pick up her book, and then cross her legs.

For a strange moment, I held my gaze, then drew back quickly. Yet even as I restrained my back upright, a distinct power was deliberately drawing me to that girl. Shoulders straight, nevertheless my head began to turn back toward her. With some effort, I held my head forward, but my eyes darted back below her desktop.

Lest any male readers be catapulted here into lustful reflection, let me say that I saw her knee. But that was quite enough long ago in this land far, far away—where high school dress codes banned girls' slacks, jeans, or shorts and required skirt hems to extend decisively in the ankle direction.

Again, for readers of the Western scientific mentality, I must note here that although a manifest power had palpably seized my body, no one was touching me. I knew the effects of such purely physical force, because our freshman P.E. class had recently included a unit on wrestling. Not just textbook instruction, but bones on the mat, hands gripping your arm and shoulder, muscles shoving and pulling your body.

The young lady of my focus, however—and you must trust me on this—had not climbed down and across the row of desks between us, seized my head and shoulders, and drawn me toward her. So far as I could tell—and hoped—she never even knew I looked.

Untouched yet impacted, I sat uneasily as my heartbeat skipped into high gear. Suddenly, the room felt warmer. Far too soon afterward, the bell rang and everyone jumped up to run out to their next class but me. After some very nonchalant if fearful dawdling, eventually I was able to stand and exit with some dignity.

Stressful as this experience was for me, the worst and arguably the most significant part of the story happened later—or rather, didn't happen.

Arriving home from school, I went out to the local sandlot and played baseball with my friends, came back, then watched some TV til Dad came home from work. Eventually, my father, mother, two sisters, and I sat around the table and ate dinner together. Afterward, while my mom and sisters cleaned up in the kitchen, I took out the trash, went in my room to do homework, watched some more TV, then took a shower and went to bed.

WHAT'S MISSING?

Quick: What's missing from this picture? If you don't know, this demonstrates how our culture has become blinded to the roots of sexuality for a man and the ordained source of security amid its unsettling, literally proverbial mysteries.

Why, when the female family contingent was in the kitchen, did I not go to my father and cry out, "Dad, help! I got hit by a ton of bricks today in algebra class! You must know something about this or I wouldn't be standing here in front of you. My whole body got all hot and... Is that OK?

"Dad—am *I* OK?"

If the response when I tell this story at men's conferences is any indication, few of us men today went freely to our fathers for help as boys when sexual attraction first invaded our bodies and minds.

Why not?

"Too embarrassing" might summarize the majority of responses. But why is it embarrassing for a boy to talk about a normal bodily function, especially to a man who not only has a demonstrable amount of experience with it, but is in fact the man closest to him? Part of the problem may be simply that parents have not been taught themselves beyond the mechanics of sex, so cannot tell either son or daughter about its roots, purpose, and fulfillment.

Certainly, many boys do not grow up trusting and feeling close to their fathers, who may be absent either physically or emotionally (see *Sons of the Father: Healing the Father-Wound in Men Today*). Beyond that interpersonal dynamic, however, we must ask: Is there something inherent to sexuality that makes it hard to communicate openly about it?

One answer may lie in its very nature. If indeed sexual attraction is at root a *super*-natural event, it proclaims thereby the weakness of our mere natural human faculties. When nobody talks openly and safely about such overwhelming power, the vacuum can threaten shame (see "Overcoming Spiritual Denial" in *Religion vs Reality*).

Indeed, if sexuality is fundamentally a spiritual phenomenon, why has presumably the most manifest spiritual community among us—the Church—not taught us about it? Why unto today are we vastly ignorant about so pervasive a power, which has permeated life since our very genesis as a species?

Mystery—with all its uncertainty and fear, excitement and promise—abounds here, as anyone with a mustard grain of honesty knows.

By definition, the spirit realm hosts *super*-natural forces far greater than our natural human perception and strength. As a spiritual phenomenon, therefore, sexual desire stirs with a warning: "Caution: You are about to enter the spirit realm. Forces you will engage after this point are beyond your ability to control."

At the same time, we know that sexuality beckons the very power of creation itself.

With that warning and that promise, we proceed here both humbly and hopefully.

> Today's youth may be the most sexually exposed generation in history—and by no coincidence, the first for whom sexuality has become more of a burden than a joy.

1

Sexual Rabbit Trails

The Season of Return

If someone misses the road, doesn't he turn back? Why then, my people, do you turn away from me without ever turning back?...

The stork in the sky knows the time to migrate, the dove and the swift and the wryneck know the season of return; but my people do not know the ordinances of the Lord. Jer. 8:4,5TEV, :7NEB

YEARS AGO WHEN MY SON was a boy, we enjoyed hiking together in the forests and creek beds of the nearby Santa Ynez mountains. Uninspired by common main paths, soon after leaving the trailhead we would search for "rabbit trails"—those smaller diversions promising more adventure amid the poison oak, slippery rocks, and unyielding scrub brush.

Sooner or later, our off-trail expeditions would lead us to a dead end in the woods, with not so much as a dent in the undergrowth to guide us onward. At that point, with the two of us standing confused and shuffling uncertain in the leaves, the boy would look up at me with furrowed brow and plead, "Where are we, Daddy?"

Real men, of course, don't get lost—but we do become uncertain of our position at times. "Well, son," I would sigh, not without a hint of shame, "I don't really know just where we are. But if we can get back to the trailhead, we'll be OK."

SEXUAL RABBIT TRAILS

The "social revolution" of recent decades has beckoned popular culture onto a limitless variety of sexual rabbit trails. From pornography, adultery, and casual "hooking up" to gender confusion, epidemic Sexually Transmitted Disease (STD), and prime-time affairs, our diversions have led us off the beaten path deep into a sexual wilderness.

To a young man, the forest of attraction is rife with both fear and excitement, thereby promising great adventure. Sooner or later, he's determined to enter it. The very impetus of physical maturity compels it—even though all too often, the emotional and spiritual maturity which shepherds it has rarely been demonstrated or instilled.

At a recent men's conference in the US, for example, I asked 125 men "When you were 11 or 12, did your dad talk to you helpfully about girls and sex?" Only two said Yes. Later, in France, I asked sixty French men that same question via a trustworthy translator, and not one hand went up.

Similar responses at my conferences from Los Angeles to Boston, from Hong Kong to South Africa, have led me to believe that today sexual ignorance is virtually universal—and not just among youth.

Insofar as the male sperm cell carries the x-y chromosome variant while the female carries the uniform x-x, the father determines gender identity in the child. This paternal biological imperative has manifest emotional consequences as well. The epidemic lack of fathering today has prompted widespread gender confusion in both men and women (see "Fathers and Daughters" in *Healing the Masculine Soul* and "Homosexuality and the Father Wound" in *Religion vs Reality*).

On the threshold of virility, a young man hears powerful and at times overwhelming voices calling him to enter the sexual forest. Where is the father to greet him with a hearty "Welcome, son!"—?

Indeed, where is the older man to say, "Our Father God has given us this marvelous desire to know and embrace the woman. In order to appreciate and enjoy it fully, you must beware the diversions and dangers that lurk here. But if you stay with me, I'll teach you how this power was designed to function and how to fulfill its purpose"—?

Later, as the trail requires discipline and restraint, the young man pauses before a flowing stream. "This journey is hard," he complains. "My body wants water. I'm going to take a drink here."

Where is the old man to intervene, "Wait a minute, son. Don't drink from that stream!"—?

"Why not?" the young man protests. "The water looks perfectly clear."

"Yes, I know your body wants water and this stream appears clean to your physical senses. But you must trust me. That water contains micro-organisms which *your natural human faculties can't perceive*. One drink and your intestines will remember it for a long time. I know you're thirsty and I will provide healthy water for you."

"But where?"

The old man gestures ahead, pointing upwards.

The young man balks. "That looks like a tough climb!"

"Yes, son, you got that right," the elder affirms. "It *is* a tough journey. But trust me: it's worth it. What's more, I'll get you there."

Further along the trail, the young man pauses when his eye is distracted off to the side. "I see something over there that looks exciting!" he exclaims. "I'm going off the trail to see more."

Where is the credible manly voice to say, "Hold on, son! I know it looks wonderful and feels powerful. But moss grows on the cliff top there and if you get too close, you'll slide off the edge and fall. I can tell you, it *is* exciting. What's more, in good time, you'll see all of it and be blessed beyond measure—if you persevere with me on the trail"—?

WOUND IN WOMEN

The same father-wound leads women to devalue themselves and choose relationships which reinforce a low self-image. As 26-year-old author Wendy Shalit noted in *A Return to Modesty,*

> When I talk to women my age and hear…
> the kind of treatment they put up with from
> these boyfriends of theirs, the first thing I ask
> them is, "Does your father know about this?"
> They look at me as if I'm from another planet.
> Of course their fathers don't know.[3]

In addition to father-absence, a growing mother-wound in women today has also inflicted daughters and their sense of femininity. Many men want very much to know what's happening in their daughters' lives, but feel inadequate to engage. "I want to be a good dad to my daughter," as one man at a conference told me, "but I don't know how. What does a girl need from her father?"

"I don't have a daughter myself," I told him. "But your wife is a daughter with a father. Ask her what she needed from her dad when she was your daughter's age."

The next day, he reported: "I asked my wife what she needed from her dad when she was a girl. She just kind of shook her head like she was sad and said, 'I don't know'."

Intrigued, I pressed him. "What does that tell you about your wife, brother?"

"I guess," he sighed, "she never got it."

Since that time years ago, I've challenged women around the world after my men's conferences to devise a program together to teach every dad in their church what his daughter needs from him. "We men love our daughters and want to be good dads," I've urged them. "Please, we need you to tell us how to do that."

Sadly, tragically, the women just withdraw and abandon their daughters even as they themselves were abandoned as girls. Only one church out of hundreds, long ago in England in 1997, has told me that their women took up this challenge to educate fathers in behalf of their daughters.

I ask women, "When you first became attracted to boys, did your mother talk to you about the great power you now have not only to turn a man's head but to influence his heart?" The women respond with blank stares, often with a hint of sadness and fear—and a longing for a mother's guidance themselves.

Mind you, *these are Christian audiences*, communities of faith with access to the Creator of life itself. These men and women read the Bible, listen to sermons every week, pray to the true God, and see themselves ordained as salt and light to this dark and fallen world (Matt. 5:13,14).

Amid the power of sexuality, however, they cower as ignorant, fearful, and lost.

Without credible mentoring, both men and women today— Christian or not—have become disoriented and misled, with no trodden groove in the forest landscape to suggest a hospitable path ahead. Trembling beneath a veneer of either liberal sophistication or conservative control, increasingly our hearts cry out to the Creator of sexuality, "Father, where are we?"

SEXUAL OVERLOAD

Historically, today's popular "sexual liberation" movement first gained traction with the adolescent Boomers of the 1960s, who entered the world as their parents were casting off the self-restraints mandated by World War II. Launched amid the gas-guzzling excesses of the 1950s, Boomers grew up to shed not only material deprivation but sexual deprivation as well. From hip-swinging Elvis to fornication and homosexuality, the children of the WWII warriors swung the pendulum from historically accepted norms to a broad array of sexual expression.

Being exposed to so much power without knowing how to focus it safely, however, stirs a fear which trumps its pleasure.

Today, after decades of dismissing boundaries, a younger generation of men and women often feel overloaded and confused—and are having second thoughts. The popular promise of unbounded sexual gratification has disappointed, leaving them not free, but rather, trapped between the shame-full "conservative/judgmental" past and the shame-less "liberal/ tolerant" present—with no apparent alternative.

"Don't do it," the old religion warns. "Remember the wages of sin or you'll be shamed and punished!"

"Just do it," the happening media urges. "Forget your conscience and heart. Don't miss out on all the fun!"

Struggling between these competing voices has left youth either sexually de-sensitized and burned out or hyper-sensitized and addicted. They're tired not only of being shamed and inhibited by the demands of judgmental morality, but also of being abandoned and disillusioned by the careless indulgence of "tolerant acceptance."

"Modern" Western culture, meanwhile, has become incapable of hosting a dialog which might reveal other, healthy options. In fact, we've abdicated our own scientific heritage and retreated not only from honest truth-seeking but from genuine respect of others.

Views are called "different," after all, because they contain beliefs that are not compatible with other views. To avoid conflict and offense, we enforce the aloof, universalist position that all views are equally valid. But this disengaged stance requires in effect that no views are ultimately valid—which only leaves everyone not enlightened, but rather, invalidated, patronized, and offended (see "Spiritual Imperialism: Secularization and White Racism" in *Religion vs Reality*).

Shameless tolerance has supplanted shameful morality. Fearing truth that would upend our unassailable, inoffensive worldview and lacking any option beyond returning to moral judgment, we've abdicated both our hearts and our bodies. We've doused a burning passion for what's ultimately real with the cold waters of religion and ideology.

In the absence of a credible alternative, relationships between men and women today are increasingly tentative, painful, and discouraging. A younger generation, at least two thirds of whom have suffered their parents' divorce, is at best cautious about relational commitment. Interactions, from quick hookups and "friends with benefits" to online social media connections, are deliberately if not desperately shallow.

In a news feature "The curse of the hookup culture," New York University professor Jonathan Zimmerman notes that

> The culture is marked by a lack of commitment and especially of communication between partners, who rarely tell each other what they want. So it has brought with it an appalling amount of unwanted sex.... Students feel a great deal of pressure to keep the sex casual, that is, to remove themselves emotionally from it....

> What most students of both sexes really
> want—as my own students often tell me—is a
> long-standing, romantic relationship. But the
> hookup code works against that, encouraging
> them to remain isolated and detached.[4]

Meanwhile, hearts are breaking, marriages are imploding, and gender confusion is becoming the norm.

It's overwhelming. Today's youth, in fact, may be the first generation in history in which sexual boundaries have virtually been eliminated—and by no coincidence, for whom sexuality has become more of a burden than a joy.

The spiritual essence of sexuality prompts several common responses to this dilemma. Christians may seek refuge in a religious spirit from the sensual overload and confusion, and urge a return to restrictive, shame-bound "biblical Law." Others more secularized swallow the bait wholesale and fall headlong into an unbounded lustful spirit via promiscuity and/or pornography.

Still others simply drop out, abdicating their sexuality altogether to an asexual spirit via an androgynous or "metrosexual" lifestyle. "I'm a conscientious objector in the war between the sexes," as *Doonesbury* comic strip's perennial Boomer adolescent Zonker declared.

SEXUAL CHAOS

Amid the escalating chaos, we've learned to respect the power of sexuality not only to uplift and create, but also to consume and destroy—from STD-infected bodies to shattered hearts. Nevertheless, in spite of our addictive culture and our own broken human nature, men and women today still struggle hopefully after mutual respect and enduring love in a relationship.

Like the birds whose migratory instincts Jeremiah appreciates in the opening scripture above, we know when the forbidding chill of religion prompts us to leave for warmer climes more hospitable to the human heart. Yet we justly fear the hot, untamed jungle.

These false yet seductive spiritual detours beg the central question for today: Does the God revealed in Jesus offer any genuine alternative to men and women who yet struggle to honor their hearts and bodies?

Even as a homing instinct, we long for another destination more authentic to our heritage and destiny. Unlike the birds, however, we've forgotten where lie the green pastures and still waters that restore our souls (see Ps. 23:2).

Without a credible alternative, liberation becomes an end in itself. In battling to be liberated *from* repressive parental, cultural, and religious shame, the 1960s rebels dissociated from God and thereby, forgot what we long to be liberated *for*. Dismissing traditional values, the culture fled law for license—only to discover that neither law *nor* license respects our heartfelt longing for loving relationship.

As both the cold warnings of morality and the steamy promises of license increasingly dissatisfy, we wonder, even beg: Is there not another option? Can men and women both respect and celebrate our sexuality? Can we not focus authentically on its created purpose even as we enjoy its pleasures?

I'm not calling here for either re-enforced morality or un-enforced license. Rather, I'm urging that we renounce both as a distraction from God's call to genuine manhood and womanhood. It's time, in fact, to remember the One who created us "male and female in His image," so that divine intention might be distinguished and rescued from today's compelling counterfeits.

That's what this book is about, namely, exposing the world's false promises—often from both the "traditional" *and* "liberation" camps— in order to re-discover the true origin, nature, and destiny of sexual desire. From that trailhead of authenticity, men and women can begin to walk safely in the adventure of attraction and experience the fulfillment we long for—indeed, for which we were created.

WHO-TO BOOK

Amid so many self-help guides today, distinctions are in order.

This is not a "how-to" book, but rather, a "who-to" book. It's not about "what you can do to improve your sex life," but rather, what God is doing to accomplish His purposes in men and women today and how He provides what you need to join Him.

It's neither a righteous exhortation to seize after "moral values" nor a siren call to shed inhibitions. It's the cry of a Father who longs not to deprive us of pleasure but rather, to save us from pain. In fact, He loves His children so much that He's designed protective boundaries for us. What's more, He wants so badly for us to enjoy His freedom and blessing as sons and daughters that He's poured out the power of His Spirit to walk safely within those boundaries.

"I will give you a new heart and put a new spirit in you," the God who created sexual desire has promised us in His New Covenant via Jesus:

> *I will remove* from you your heart of stone and give you a heart of flesh. And *I will put* my Spirit in you and move you to follow my decrees and be careful to keep my laws. You will live in the land I gave your forefathers; you will be my people and I will be your God. (Ezek. 36:26-28NIV, italics mine)

What you read here is not about the Tree of the Knowledge of Good and Evil. It's not a clinic on "knowing right from wrong," but rather, a family journey in knowing the Father's heart for His children. It's not a commandment to obey, but rather, an invitation to trust. It's not about trying harder to measure up to principles of behavior, no matter how biblically based or even manifestly beneficial.

Rather, it's about the Tree of Life, that is, surrendering to the God who has come in Jesus for those real enough to confess they *can't* measure up (see Romans 7:18-8:1). It's about a Father determined to save His children from the brokenness of this world and recruit us to overcome it in others—a Father who wants to give His children the very best and won't rest until we recognize it as such and receive it freely.

In fact, the God who created desire has come in Jesus to promote authentic sexual freedom.

In the world, "free sex" means no boundaries or restrictions on its expression. Maturity, however, grows when you've suffered the brokenness of this world in your own heart, often through failed relationship and humbly facing your own shortcomings that contributed to it.

Eventually, you realize that your natural desires have trapped you so that you're unable—that is, *not* free—to walk within the safe boundaries which Father God has so graciously revealed to us. Contrary to the world's seductive promise, your flesh in fact binds you from pursuing and maintaining what you really want, namely, a committed, loving relationship.

From this renewed perspective, sexual freedom is not the absence of restriction, but the presence of the Father who enables its created purpose. Under His protection and guidance, you can at last focus your sexual energies authentically—that is, toward fulfilling your destiny surrendered to Him.

Such genuine freedom is hard wrought. It's not gained simply by shedding boundaries. You're not "free" to play the piano, for example, until you've spent time and energy practicing.

Thus, the old joke in which after successful hand surgery a patient asks his surgeon, "Can I play the piano now?"

"Yes, your hands are now fine," the surgeon reassures.

"That's great!" the patient exclaims. "I've never played the piano before."

You're not free to grow in loving relationship until you've done the hard work to heal your brokenness that sabotages it and to practice the love which undergirds it. That work includes seeking Father God's forgiveness for turning away from Him, His healing for your emotional wounds, and the deliverance which secures both.

From this perspective, the unfettered lifestyle in which the world promises "liberation" is revealed in fact as bondage, keeping you unfocused, unprepared, unproductive, and unfulfilled. Genuine freedom no longer lies in being able to seize whatever you want whenever you want it, but rather, at last to give Father God what He wants—namely, your whole self. In that process, He can renew your heart and focus your energies on fulfilling the desires He's placed within it (see Psalm 37:4).

As Paul urged the Christians in Rome,

> Offer your bodies as living sacrifices, holy and pleasing to God—which is your spiritual worship. Do not conform any longer to the pattern of this world, but be transformed by the renewing of your mind. Then you will be able to test and approve what God's Will is—his good, pleasing, and perfect will. (Rom. 12:1,2NIV)

Religion warns that you *must* focus your sexual energies on a lifelong marriage partner. Jesus promises that you *can* do so at last, even amid the awful brokenness in this world and thereby, in yourself. Surrendered to and trusting Him, a man and woman can experience genuine freedom to grow together as "suitable companions" in God's purposes (Gen. 2:18).

There's Good News here for those who remain so humble and so hopeful:

The season of return has come.

It's time to go back to the Trailhead.

For a man, the innate human longing to go home focuses in this world upon the woman's womb. His eyes search after it and his body longs to return there.

2

Holy Nostalgia

Sexual Desire as Homesickness

Each of these people of faith died not yet having in hand what was promised, but still believing. How did they do it? They saw it way off in the distance, waved their greeting, and accepted the fact that they were transients in this world. People who live this way make it plain that they are looking for their true home. Hebrews 11:13-14TMB

"WHERE ARE YOU FROM?" seems a simple question for most people, but it always intimidated me as a military brat. My father, a career Navy officer, literally took me around the world with our family, from my birthplace in Philadelphia to Columbus, OH; to Washington, DC; to Karachi, Pakistan; to Norfolk, VA.

Brats: Our Journey Home, a DVD "documentary about growing up military," portrays poignantly both the adventure and heartache of being a military child.[5] I learned early, as the film notes, "what it's like to feel like an outsider in your own country" and "struggle to fit in." The subtitle says it all: "Because everybody needs a home."

This lack of worldly roots stirred in me a deep longing to feel centered. That unfocused homesickness led me at 40 to visit my father's birthplace outside Philadelphia—from which his dad, my grandfather born in 1880, never traveled more than 75 miles in his lifetime (see "Boots for a Working Man" in *Healing the Masculine Soul*). Eventually, I discovered that my Dalbey surname comes from Norway and visited that country for several weeks.

During my Norwegian sojourn, I learned the language, soaked in the culture, and began for the first time to enjoy a sense of ethnic identity (see "Norwegian Bivouac" in *No Small Snakes: A Journey into Spiritual Warfare*). One evening, a group of Christian friends near Oslo prayed for me. As they did, amid words of *kraft* (power), *styrke* (strength), and *hjemmelengst* (lit. "home longing"), I was startled to hear in my mind the English words, *You have found your home.*

Excitedly, my heart leapt. *Thank you, Father God!* I exclaimed in prayer. *So you want me to leave California and come to live here in Norway?*

Gently, the response came: *Wherever people love and serve me, there is your home.*

With that simple statement, my search for worldly roots ended.

And yet....

At last, I could now answer the question, "Where are you from?" I confess, however, that the revelation of my Norwegian origins in this world—even as it focused me on the deeper fellowship of God's people— did not wholly satisfy my longing for a home. To answer The Question authentically, in fact, we must begin with the more foundational issue, Where does life begin?

Geographically, the Bible marks the genesis of humanity in the Garden of Eden, aka Paradise. All of us come, that is, from a place of perfection, of pristine order sustained by divine intention—"excellent in every way" according to the Bible (Gen. 1:31LIV). Here, the Creator fashioned not only plants and animals, but His final and crowning achievement, humankind—in Hebrew, *Adam.*

LONGING FOR HOME

As the New Testament letter to the Hebrews implies in the opening text above, every human being unto today has an innate longing to go home. Like Jeremiah's migrating birds, each of us wants to return to your place of origin, where your identity was first cast. As such, "Home Sweet Home" beckons the immeasurable blessing of belonging, provision, and security.

Although—or likely, because—Boomers famously sought to cut off from their parents, popular songs from that era often focused on going home.

John Denver's "Take Me Home, Country Roads" hinted at the basic mother-connection in his refrain "West Virginia, mountain mama." Paul Simon's "Homeward Bound" took the next logical step in focusing on the woman partner, as, "I wish I was/Homeward bound/Home where my love lies waitin'/silently for me."

While white Boomers were renouncing their politically incorrect heritage and severing headlong from their history, African-Americans were leading a more authentic journey of rediscovery. Thus, black author Alex Haley's book *Roots*, tracing his cultural history to slavery and West Africa, became a bestseller and prize-winning TV series.

Nevertheless, singer Joe South's poignant 1968 "Don't It Make You Want to Go Home"[6] lamented how the longing to return to geographic roots in this world is so often disappointed. After "a long, long time," he goes back to his home town, only to discover that there's a freeway by the creek where he "went skinny dippin' as a child," and a drive-in theater covers the old meadow where "strawberries used to grow wild."

"All God's children get weary when they roam," he sings, then repeats over and again, "Don't it make you wanna go home?"

As a dislocated military brat, I can testify that indeed, it does. The problem, however, as this song portrays so graphically, is that your childhood locale never measures up to your golden expectations.

You Can't Go Home Again, as novelist Tom Wolfe's 1940 bestseller of that title lamented:

> You can't go back home to your family, back
> home to your childhood, back home to romantic
> love, back home to a young man's dreams of
> glory and of fame,… away from all the strife and
> conflict of the world, back home to the father
> you have lost and have been looking for, back
> home to someone who can help you, save you,
> ease the burden for you, back home to the old
> forms and systems of things which once seemed
> everlasting but which are changing all the time—
> back home to the escapes of Time and Memory.

Certainly, this disconnect from your earthly roots threatens your sense of identity and security. "Loneliness," Wolfe concludes, "far from being a rare and curious phenomenon, is the central and inevitable fact of human existence."[7]

Even if your childhood family was dysfunctional and painful, nevertheless the longing to go home remains fixed in your human nature. It's eminently natural. Organically, your mother and father therefore guard the gateway to this journey of ultimate self-discovery beyond your worldly roots. It can only proceed, therefore, insofar as you deliberately seek healing for your childhood emotional and spiritual wounds.

FAMILY IDOLATRY

Those who don't face the idolatry amid their family loyalties often indulge it with racism, nationalism, and other ingrown fortifications, never growing beyond their childhood worldview or parochial values. Others attempt to elevate themselves above the confusion and pains of life with sophistry, fancying that they're world citizens "above it all." Both of these worldly options, either to immerse or disengage, disallow the innate longing for a more authentic connection and centering—that is, for the biblical "true home" from where humanity itself comes.

The major problem on the journey to maturity and destiny is not that we want to go home, but that we naturally center that desire on an earthly locale—and are thereby perpetually disappointed. We fixate our lives on Mom and Dad, never leaving them by either capitulating to their values or rejecting them. Meanwhile, insofar as all human parents are imperfect, no worldly home—whether you run toward it or away from it—can fulfill the perfect, archetypal human vision.

Joe South and Tom Wolfe were right. You can go back to the natural territory, but it's never the same as the childhood fantasy in your heart. That's both disappointing and painful. It's also fearful, because the organic longing to go home never disappears.

It makes you wonder: When the world's focus has been revealed as false, where is the true one?

This essential confession and its humble cry drive honest men and women back to the Trailhead. There, at last, we can cry out to God for His centering, saving hand. Insofar as we thereby challenge our childish fantasy and grieve the loss of our natural home, we become eligible for the reward of ultimate reality—namely, a glimpse of our authentic, *super*natural home.

In this present, fallen world, therefore, we're literally forever dissatisfied and uncentered, "looking for our true home." The above mentioned pop songs and many others like them, harken unto that vision. Secular songwriters, however, can't portray it authentically because they don't know the God on whom it ultimately focuses.

This widely adored myopia has profound sexual implications. Whether we choose to deny or celebrate it, we're creatures of spirit, longing for our spiritual home. In a blindly secularized culture like ours, sexual desire becomes vastly overemphasized, since it serves as the only natural and intentional access to the spirit realm—as apart from unbidden dreams or ingested drugs. As such, it bears the major burden of connection to the most fundamental reality of life.

PANTHEON OF LUST

A people who fear and refuse to embrace authentic spiritual reality will therefore be embraced by sexual addiction and effectively worship sexual desire—much as other, ancient pagans. This pantheon of lust is portrayed in the Old Testament Baal cult of Canaan and the New Testament Aphrodite cult of Corinth—and mirrored in today's enticing celebrity cult of Hollywood.

Authentic, healthy sexuality, meanwhile, begins with knowing the true God of creation revealed in Israel, who has been made accessible to us in Jesus, and is now active among us today in Holy Spirit. This God not only created sexual desire, but the spiritual and physical universe which hosts it.

Even as we all want to go back where we came from, therefore, a memory chip in the human hard drive designates Eden as our common heritage and default longing. Without this larger, spiritual focus, we're left with no primal connectedness, abandoned and lost amid the terminal loneliness which author Wolfe portrays—and which the human heart knows all too well.

From a biblical view, however, the God who created this world has not only acknowledged that inherent loneliness in the natural world, but provided masterfully to overcome its misfocus on Mom and Dad. Thus, the Genesis story of creation explicitly links this longing for a more authentic home with sexual desire: "a man will *leave his father and mother and be united to his wife,* and they will become one flesh" (Gen. 2:24NIV, italics mine).

Home as defined by Mom and Dad is thereby marked as a worldly idol, which distracts from your primal, "true home" in Father God's purposes. Mature adulthood requires turning away from your parents' home and toward God's ordained, unique place for you in this world.

Marriage spurs this maturity, because the union of male and female reflects the image of God. Sexual desire—that is, becoming "one flesh" with your spouse—consummates it both in creating a new family and in centering you as "suitable companions" in God's calling instead of your parents'. Yes, we're commanded to "honor your mother and father," but not to focus your life on them and honor their call over God's.

ALONE OR LONELY?

Certainly, the Father has created each man and woman as an individual in a single body. In that sense, *aloneness* defines our created state of being in this world and is about what God has done. *Loneliness,* contrary to author Tom Wolfe's popular view, is not an "inevitable fact of human existence," but rather the consequence of human choice. It stems from what we have done, namely, the dark emptiness we host when we deny our state of aloneness and harbor its insecurity.

"Loneliness"—as Mary defines it—is therefore "The natural human state of aloneness when not acknowledged and surrendered to Father God."

Relationships become mutually supportive as each partner finds strength and security in Father God, that is, insofar as you allow the pain and fear of aloneness to drive you to Him for primary relationship. "Help me, Father!" you can pray. "I don't like being so alone! Please, draw me close to you so I can be truly centered—and dare to draw close to another person without fear of losing myself." Surrendered to Father God and His guidance, both partners are saved from worshipping each other to worship Him, to receive and share the resources of His Spirit, and thereby to fulfill His larger purposes for them together.

Under God's Kingdom rule, "surrendered" does not imply passivity, as simply pulling the covers over your head and waiting for Him to do everything. Rather, it means actively preparing yourself for life's challenges by drawing close to the Father and having done your best, moving ahead and trusting Him for the outcome. Similarly, a warrior "surrenders" first to the superior officer, who equips the troops for battle in boot camp. Thus prepared, the soldier steps out onto the battlefield to fight—even as thus prayed up, you move into life's challenges and conflict.

Now that we've exposed our natural, worldly home as inadequate, if not counterfeit, we're ready to move from the historical/geographic question to its organic counterpart: Where in the natural world does bodily life universally originate? In what physical place, that is, do all of us begin our lives?

The genesis of human life, of course, takes place in no city or earth-bound geographic locale, but rather, in the mother's womb. Thus, even as birds migrate back to their original nesting area and salmon to the stream where they were spawned, human beings want to return *in utero*.

CONTAINED BY MOM

Being contained by Mother, in fact, is the closest thing to Eden in this world. In that place, presumably, all needs are met. There, we were secured and protected, kept warm and fed even without asking, unaware of and thereby untroubled by any other world. In the womb, we live like Adam and Eve at the outset, enjoying a state of primal security, provision, and innocence with no striving to perform—nor knowledge of good and evil.

That's why we commonly associate Mom with home, even as a surrogate, indeed counterfeit Tree of Life. As such, she is the primary temptation to idolatry in this world—to be honored, but not worshipped. (see "Out from the Womb" in *Healing the Masculine Soul* and "Cutting the Cord: A Second Postpartum" in *Sons of the Father*).

Of course, no human being can shrink back to an embryonic size and re-situate in your mother's womb. Thus, when Jesus tells Nicodemus "No one can see the Kingdom of God unless he is born again," this leader of the Pharisees is mystified.

"How can a grown man be born again?" Nicodemus exclaims. "He certainly cannot enter his mother's womb and be born a second time!"

But of course, Jesus is talking here about a *super*-natural re-birth, even a new identity as a child of Father God made possible by His Spirit:

> "I am telling you the truth," replied Jesus,
> "that no one can enter the Kingdom of God
> unless he is born of water and the Spirit. A
> person is born physically of human parents, but
> spiritually of the Spirit." (John 3:3-5)

(see "A Time to Die, a Time to Be Born—Again" in *Broken by Religion, Healed by God*).

Yet, between the physical experience of being born of your mother's womb and the spiritual experience of being born again as a son or daughter of Father God, another intermediate reality beckons. Maybe, indeed, a man *can* re-enter the womb and therein experience the Father's power to create a new life—even a life like unto himself.

In the act of sexual intercourse, that is, he can experience a renewal of his spirit and even conceive a new life in his child. The experience of being "born again" of the Spirit may be celebrated in the "one flesh" union of husband and wife surrendered to Jesus—or counterfeited in sex outside that commitment and therefore apart from your created destiny.

With that statement, I confess the limit of my understanding. Such is the mystery of life.

Nevertheless, significant observations may be noted here.

THE WOMB AS EDEN

I cannot speak for women. For a man, however, the woman's womb is as Eden. A man's homesickness for roots—his longing to be rejuvenated, re-centered, and returned to Paradise—focuses on re-entering the woman's body sexually even as he entered his mother's body via conception.

Scripture enshrines the human body as the "temple of the Spirit" (1 Corinth. 6:19). As such, the woman's womb is the Holy of holies. It's the most sacred place in this natural world, set apart by the Creator God to do His finest work in bringing forth humanity—even as He did in Eden. In entering the woman's body, the man acts like God more graphically than in any other human enterprise. Yet again, even now, creation takes place as he ventures via flesh into eternity, sparking life in her womb even as Father God conceived humanity in The Garden.

Significantly, in ancient Israel entering the temple Holy of holies implied intimate and direct confrontation with God. Only the High Priest ordained by God was therefore allowed to do so, and then only upon diligent cleansing and preparation.

Amid such overwhelming power, this task was understood to be life-threatening—like risking a great supernatural jolt of electricity beyond the human body's natural ability to absorb. In fact, ancient temple attendants tied a rope to the High Priest's foot before he entered the Holy of holies, so his body could be dragged out should he faint or die confronting God there. Unto today, Orthodox Jews in Israel are forbidden to visit the Jerusalem Temple mount, for fear they might inadvertently step into that most sacred spot and suffer the awful consequences of not being cleansed and prepared to do so.

Similarly, the marriage covenant implies that the husband is the High Priest who alone is ordained by God to enter the holy place of his wife's womb. There, in sexual intercourse, he experiences the voltage of creation, and in that sense, encounters the Creator God.

Accordingly, he had better be cleansed and wholly prepared for the consequences—both marvelous if properly respected and terrible if not. Indeed, what married couple has not fought fiercely and later forgiven each other—and then found a new passion and joy, even healing, in making love afterwards? On the other hand, as we'll see later, demonic powers lurk when this reality is disregarded (Ch 10, "What God Has Joined Together: Spiritual Consequences of Physical Union").

Sexual intercourse, therefore, is no trifling matter, no mere response to "animal magnetism" between physical bodies. By virtue of its spiritual impetus, it might well be called the most "awe-filled" experience afforded to human beings.

Every man who enters the woman's womb acts as the High Priest; every woman, as the Holy of holies. At the very least, this revelation should stir in the man and the woman a reverence for the privilege of sexual union, a mutual respect for each others' bodies, and a determination to honor sexual boundaries which demonstrate that reverence and that respect. A couple's abstaining from sex before marriage is not about being morally or religiously correct, but rather, protecting themselves from the risk of mishandling such spiritual power.

The consummate blessing of sexual desire is therefore reserved for those who rejoice in the overwhelming promise it beckons and humbly abide its warnings. For a man and woman, that means seeking the spiritual and emotional healing that both need in order to "leave father and mother" before becoming "one flesh" in marriage.

If the man has not broken the emotional tie to his mother, his sexual desire for his wife will be hijacked by his boyhood longing for Mom. He'll see—and judge—his wife through the lens of his boyhood experience with Mom. He'll find it hard to see or enjoy his wife as the woman she truly is. Not seeing his partner clearly can truncate his destiny with her.

HOLY NOSTALGIA

Even now, that is, an organic longing both physical and spiritual compels a man to return to the womb, to the authentic origin of his natural life—in order to enjoy the holy ecstasy of Creation and be refreshed by its restored innocence. His vision is thereby drawn to that part of a woman's body.

Sexual desire is a holy nostalgia.

To a man, the woman is portable Paradise, like the Ark of the Covenant. Her body contains the very context for creation, and thereby, the avenue to restoration and renewal.

Accordingly, the female pudendum is the archetypal gateway back home to Eden. A man's eyes search for it relentlessly and his very body longs to go there—in order to revisit the Paradise from whence he came.

In spite of religion's best efforts to repress and obscure this reality, the world knows and proclaims it—from miniskirts to low-rise women's jeans. "Treat me like an angel and I'll take you to heaven," as one bumper sticker I saw on a woman driver's car put it.

Similarly, the late crooner Nat King Cole's 1950's hit "Paradise" made the quintessential point:

And when she holds my hand/That's when I understand:

Her eyes afire/with one desire

In heavenly bliss/could I resist?

And when she dims the light/Then I hold her tight

She takes me to Paradise.[8]

I first saw the word "ecstasy"—literally, "to stand outside of," as in to elevate your senses beyond the natural world—in a pornographic magazine as a teenager. I next saw it later at college in a world religions textbook reference to worship.

Under God's authority—that is, when both partners are surrendered to Him—sexuality bears power to revisit your "true home." It thereby restores you to your authentic, original self, pure and whole like Adam in the Beginning. Under the Father's aegis, sexual intercourse re-centers you in His created purpose.

A significant catch, however, guards the gateway.

Getting back to Paradise is no cakewalk. Remember that Adam and Eve were expelled as punishment for not trusting and thereby disobeying God:

> After (God) drove the man out, he placed
> on the east side of the Garden of Eden cherubim
> and a flaming sword flashing back and forth to
> guard the way to the tree of life. (Gen. 3:24NIV)

Contrary to cute Sunday School images, the Hebrew *cherubim* refers not to chubby, smiling little babies, but rather, to large and imposing warrior angels. Like a giant fiery propeller, their "flaming sword flashing back and forth" is an intimidating show-stopper on the return trail to Eden.

Remember, the Tree of the Knowledge of Good and Evil detoured humanity away from Paradise. The Tree of Life, meanwhile, is The Way back—namely, Jesus, whose death and resurrection has bridged the chasm of sin between us and Father God, restored our innocence, and welcomed us into His heart. Thereby, He alone has made it possible for us to return to Paradise. Surrendered to Him, we live by the power of the Father's Spirit, nurtured by the Tree of Life. We're no longer distracted, misled, and burned out by the do's and don'ts inherent to the Tree of the Knowledge of Good and Evil.

If indeed sexual intercourse beckons that return, merely having intercourse will not get you there. On the contrary, without surrendering to Jesus and being thereby "born again" as an innocent child of "a parent who is immortal, not mortal," you're not able to trust the Father to uphold His marriage covenant (1 Peter 1:23). You and your spouse will fancy you don't need to turn to God for help together, that you can control your marriage by yourselves (see "From Love Bug to Faith" in *Healing the Masculine Soul*).

Any man or woman with a mustard grain of relationship experience knows that precisely the opposite is true. In fact, insofar as you don't surrender together to God's control, you'll try to control each other—and see your hearts slashed as with flaming swords.

Because this connection between sexuality and God's purposes is so fundamental to life, considerable effort is required to deny it. Indeed, the enemy of God and humanity is literally hell-bent to hide and distort it.

One demonic stratagem is to capitalize on this sexual power by using a woman's naked body to draw a man not to his home in God, but rather, to a false home/security/identity in the world via popular culture. Thus, the commanding secular focus on consumer products, often promising vitality and purpose much like worship.

A full-page *Newsweek* magazine ad[9], for example, pictures a sultry model, blond hair flowing down and over her otherwise bare shoulders, as with an alluring smile she extends a lit cigarette lighter.

The woman is literally ready to light your fire.

A male reader is drawn to that fire which the woman bears, not simply in her lighter, but as it stirs in his own body. Below, the caption reads, "Get in touch with your masculine side." This goal, so seductive and compelling to a fatherless generation, draws the male reader yet lower to a corner where the advertised whiskey bottle stands.

Who but the father of Lies could conceive a message so destructive to men and so denigrating to women? Only a spiritual being somehow privy to the Father's intention and hateful of His children could distort His heart for them so graphically.

The commercial association here objectifies sexuality, if not the woman herself, as a consumer product. In this prevailing cultural view, the woman's body is not the temple of the Spirit, but the gas station of the flesh. It's a recipe not only for pornography, but for sexism and even domestic violence.

Shame is intrinsic to our fallen sin-nature. We can't overcome it merely with our human ability and make ourselves right with God. That's why Jesus came, to bear our shame on the cross himself and eliminate it, so we wouldn't be separated from the Father and our calling sabotaged by it.

Unlike Jesus, the powers of this world cannot eliminate shame, but can only cover it up and thereby, exacerbate it. Unable since Easter to eliminate Jesus' saving presence, they offer instead a vast marketplace to distract from it.

Since that shame became embedded in our sexuality with Adam and Eve's fig leaves, the sense of sexual inadequacy has beckoned a vast catalog of distractions—from Viagra and whiskey among men to ankle-breaking high heels and push-up bras among women. Significantly, the word *pudendum* for the sex organ derives from the Latin meaning "to make or be ashamed."[10]

BACK TO EDEN

Amid the overwhelming mystery of sexuality, modern culture lacks humble openness to a reality deeper than the natural world allows. Even Christians who acknowledge the God who made us male and female in His image often do not trust Him to mediate sexual desire in and through us.

It's not that we lack the discipline to repress our sexuality, but that we lack the faith to embrace it as God intends. We allow our insecurities and fears to stir not only distrust in ourselves, but in God as well.

If indeed we human beings are creatures of a God "who is Spirit," then our inherent spiritual nature seeks to connect with its Source—as

Christians might do in worship, use of spiritual gifts, and prayer (John 4:24). A culture which fears spiritual reality for revealing our inadequacy, however, doesn't dare make that connection.

An urge is not quenched by denying its focus. A diligently secularized culture such as our own, that is, begs the question: If the true focus of the human longing for spiritual experience is denied, where shall that longing be entertained?

Certainly, false spiritualities such as fortune tellers and other New Age practices feed on that denial and offer counterfeit satisfaction. What's needed is a fundamentally spiritual urge/propensity/impulse that can be widely embraced, without the stigma of seeming "weird" or "spooky."

Here, in the absence of authentic spiritual focus on Father God, sexual desire has become the primary avenue for spiritual connection. This places a terrible burden upon sexuality, to play surrogate spirituality for a people who refuse to recognize and embrace God and receive His Spirit.

The powers of this world do not want us to remember our "true home." If we do, we'll find satisfaction in who we are because we'll know Whose we are. The world will no longer be able to manipulate us with its sexy models and market a counterfeit gender security with its makeup and miniskirts or guns and whiskey.

Ultimately, this cultural conspiracy to deny the organic power and holy focus of sexual desire distracts from the avenue back to Eden, which is Jesus. It thereby separates you from God and His ordained destiny in and through you.

The Hebrew word translated as "holy" means "to be set apart"— that is, for God's purposes. "For you are a people holy to the Lord your God," as Israel was reminded. "(He) has chosen you out of all the people on the face of the earth to be his people, his treasured possession" (Deut. 7:6NIV).

"Holy" is related to the word "sacred" and thereby, "*sacri*fice." To be set apart from the world requires a willingness to give up its popular esteem and pleasures. Thus, Jesus' sacrifice of his very life invites you to be set apart from the world's lies, enables you as a son/daughter to receive Father God's Spirit, and thereby empowers you to fulfill His plan for your life. To follow Jesus is to "sacri-fy" your own life, to dedicate and set it apart from the world's distractions for God's purposes.

Holiness, therefore, is not about what you don't do sexually, but about what God does with your sexuality. Only His Spirit can set your desire apart for His purposes, and only insofar as you give it to Him (see Rom. 12:1,2). Sexual holiness is not about mere abstinence, but commitment; nor simply about maintaining purity, but in persevering after God's destiny for you.

In the *sacra*ment of communion, for example, ordinary bread and wine from the store become set apart for God's purposes when con*secra*ted to manifest Jesus' body and blood. Thereby, it facilitates his presence and power. In the same way, as we allow Holy Spirit to set us apart from the spirit of this world, we see more clearly how we've been seduced by the self-centered powers of this world away from our true home in Father God's hands.

As we shall now see, from this perspective a man and a woman can recognize the path Father God has set for them and are empowered together as suitable companions to fulfill it.

> If you don't know what God made you to do in this world, how can you recognize a suitable companion to do it with you?

3

Desire and Destiny

Suitable Companions in Marriage

For we are God's workmanship, created in Christ Jesus to do good works, which God prepared in advance for us to do. Ephes. 2:10NIV

Then the Lord God said, "It is not good for the man to live alone. I will make a suitable companion to help him." Gen. 2:18

"PASTOR! GUESS WHAT?" Bright and beaming, Barry burst into my office and sank dreamily into a seat cushion. "I finally found the woman for me!"

"Well, that's just great," I allowed hospitably—though not without caution. The excitement, the energy, and the announcement were all too familiar in our fast-lane Southern California beach town. "Tell me about her," I offered.

"The chemistry is amazing!" he declared, leaning forward. "I mean, you wouldn't believe how she turns me on. With Sally, it's different from any other woman!"

I sighed slightly. "Barry," I affirmed, "it's clear there's a lot of excitement with the two of you, and I know that can be really good. But I need you to help me out here. Any number of women can turn you like that. In fact, what you described to me could just as easily come from a magazine or movie.

"What I want to know is this: is she a suitable companion?"

"'Suitable companion'?" Barry echoed. Puzzled, he sat back again, this time uneasily.

"Yes," I declared. "In the Bible story of creation God says He's going to make Adam a 'suitable companion' (Gen. 2:18). That means a woman who's been surrendered to the Lord long enough for Him to shape her for what He made her to do in this world—a woman who's committed to go with God's plan for her life."

Again, I paused—not wanting to rain on Barry's parade, but at the same time, wanting the best for him in a marriage.

"At some point, I want to ask you if Sally knows what God created her to do with her life. But what's more important to me here is, where are you, Barry? Do you know what God's called *you* to do in this world?"

His brow knit, Barry sat quietly confused. "Well, ... not exactly," he murmured.

"If you don't know what you're here to do in this world," I continued, "how are you going to recognize a 'suitable companion' to do it with you?" I then offered to meet with him to sort out this issue if he were genuinely serious with Sally.

It's true. It's simple. It's common. But it's not easy. Too often, young men and women are drawn by the power of sexual attraction and think, "This is so exciting and so powerful that it must be from God! Once we get married, He'll show us what He has planned for us."

CALL TO IDENTITY

And then, as they mature, the demands of jobs, children, and everyday problems co-opt intimacy. In growing relationships, that is, desire stirs increasingly from the character of the relationship and not just the appearance of the bodies. As the call to identity and purpose begin to outweigh physical desire, the spark fades and they wonder why. Without the excitement of sharing in a focused life, they have little in common and drift apart.

"Love is not looking into each other's eyes," as the saying goes, "but looking ahead together in the same direction."

When a man has little sense of calling or focus, he doesn't feel like a real man. He balks at inviting a woman into his life, because he has no life to invite her into. That feels shameful—a major turn-off.

Without listening for the Father's voice calling him, he hears only the call of the flesh. He never discovers his life purpose and wonders why his relationship with the woman is not what it used to be. He becomes a sucker for sexual temptation, from pornography to adultery. It's a toxic recipe for shame, fighting, wounding, and withdrawing.

While a sense of calling may of course go deeper than a paying job, nevertheless our ancestors were on the right track when they expected a man to have a job as a prerequisite to marrying. Commitment, responsibility, and some self-knowledge are thereby demonstrated. Unemployment can therefore be devastating not only to a man's self-esteem, but to his marriage as well.

Why do so many of us often balk when lifetime commitment beckons in a partner? Why do we lack the inner security and trust in Father God which allows you to say with heartfelt conviction, "Yes, this is the person I want to join with forever"?

The more basic question, rarely recognized or asked, is this: Why do so many of us today lack a sense of purpose and direction for our lives? Obviously, if you do have that sense, it's easier for you to narrow your choices for a companion.

Too often, you haven't surrendered fully to the God who created you and set your purpose at the foundations of the earth. "God has made us what we are," as the Apostle Paul proclaimed, "and in our union with Christ Jesus he has created us for a life of good deeds, which he has already prepared for us to do" (Ephes. 2:10).

God says, "Come close to me. Fellowship with other believers, fast, pray, read my Word, seek my healing and deliverance. Open your heart and make room for my Spirit. Let me show you what I'm doing in your life so you can join me. As you know and embrace this, your created purpose, you'll be able to recognize a partner who shares it.

"Trust me. The more you persevere after my calling, the more my Spirit can work in you to reveal and fulfill it."

TRUST AND SURRENDER

Trusting and surrendering to Father God as individuals will allow a couple to trust and surrender more deeply to each other. In that process, He'll draw you into a greater vulnerability and intimacy—which will turn you on long after the honeymoon, even after the kids are grown and gone.

Mary and I had learned about destiny and desire before we met. She had never been married. A beautiful, gifted woman with an MS in psychiatric nursing and a PhD in psychology, she had no lack of suitors. Ten years before we met, she gave her life to Jesus. She assumed that meant God would bring her a husband.

It did, and He did—but in His timing. First, each of us needed to be grounded in His calling.

Soon after surrendering her life to the Father, she was surprised one day while driving when He told her to pull over to the side of the road. There, He told her to finish her PhD in psychology and minister to women.

Some years later, on our second date, I took Mary to Disneyland. After a fun day together in Fantasyland, we found ourselves later that evening talking seriously about our lives.

"What's God doing in your life?" she asked me at one point. "Where do you plan to be in five years?"

I'd been on my face praying about that for a long time, so I respected her question as a reflection of her own intentionality and self-respect. I told her my vision—including writing more books, speaking at conferences, being a husband and father.

And then she told me an amazing story. A successful businessman had pursued her, and one evening on a date she asked him the "five year" question.

"I want to retire from my business," he replied, "and start a bed and breakfast in rural Idaho."

"That's wonderful," Mary said genuinely. "But it's not why God had me finish my PhD dissertation." Graciously, she blessed the man and his vision, but did not see him again.

Thereafter, before we met, she wrote her PhD dissertation on women and co-dependency. Since we've been married, she's ministered to women as a therapist at a Christian counseling center, director of a home for unwed pregnant women, and counselor to at-risk families for the child abuse prevention agency where she now works. Where possible, she speaks to women at the churches where I'm speaking to the men. Because of my own healing ministry, I'm able to offer encouragement and support when she discusses her own work. We often pray together for friends and church members. Certainly, we've worked hard together in our calling as parents.

ATTRACTION AND DESTINY

Most of us don't often think of sexual attraction and marriage as being intimately connected with a sense of calling and destiny. Yet that's largely why we get confused when looking for a future mate—and even when desire fades between you and your spouse.

God wants to draw us to a place of surrendering to Him, so He can show you what He created you to do and give you what you need to do it—including a suitable companion. The excitement of walking side by side with Him in the power and leading of His Spirit opens your heart to Him, and thereby, to one another. His excitement fills you both, makes you feel united together—and stirs a desire to consummate that.

Without surrendering to God, however, often we put the cart before the horse, elevating sexual attraction over His call. "Find the partner who turns you on," the world says, "and that will motivate you to find your life purpose."

Hence, the confusion—and heartache—when you discover you're spending so much time and energy holding a shallow relationship together that you're afraid to ask the larger, primary question, "What did God bring me here in this world to accomplish?" When the "chemistry" fades, you wonder why "this relationship isn't going anywhere"—because you never considered first where each of you was going.

The issue for Christians is not, Shall I yield to the temptations of the flesh or not? but rather, Shall I yield to the flesh or to God—that is, Can I trust that God has a purpose for me in life and will reveal and empower me in it as I surrender to Him? Indeed, Can I trust Him to bring me a suitable companion, even renew attraction in my marriage, as I pursue Him faithfully along that path?

It's not a cash-and-carry deal like, If you maintain this moral standard, if you bite the bullet long enough and don't do anything immoral, you get rewarded with the partner. Rather, God has a role for you in building His Kingdom in this world, and He can only accomplish it insofar as you're surrendered to Him.

A surgeon can't heal you until you get up on the operating table. The process of discovering your role and your gifting to fulfill it builds relationship between you and your Father. In that struggle, you learn the truth and the grace which will be required later for growing together with your partner.

It's not about complying with the Lawmaker's rules, but in trusting the Father's heart for you.

PRAY FOR THE WOMAN

Several months before I met Mary, I was praying one day and heard the Father tell me, *Pray for the woman.*

"You bet, Father!" I exclaimed. "In fact, I'll pray 'unceasingly' for a woman, like your Word says!" (1 Thess. 5:17).

Eventually, I realized He was not telling me simply to ask Him to bring me *any* woman, but rather, to intercede for "the" woman He was preparing for me. "But I don't know her, Father, I said. How am I supposed to pray for her?"

I know her, I sensed His reply, *and I want you to know her before you meet so you can recognize her and move straightaway in my purposes together.*

At that, I remembered Romans 8:34: "Christ Jesus…is at the right side of God, pleading with Him in our behalf." That meant Jesus was already praying for this woman. What's more, He wanted me to draw close enough to Him to sense how He was praying, so I could take that prayer to the Father genuinely "in the name of Jesus."

When I first began praying for "the woman," I became uneasy and nervous. Uncertain, I prayed further and realized that she herself was uneasy and nervous, and God had shown me that graphically by letting me experience it. From that perspective, I could see that He wanted me to pray against that in her, namely, for her comfort, security, and confidence. That's how the Father introduced me to Mary—and began bonding me to her before we ever met.

Months later, after we met, I showed Mary my journal with the date written by each entry.

"That's amazing!" she exclaimed. "That first day you prayed for me was the day I went in for my PhD oral exams! I was nervous, alright, and definitely needed that support." Mary did well on her exams and received her degree.

To my single brothers and sisters, I say: Don't waste your energy complaining about being single and alone. Focus it instead on preparing for your partner by 1) seeking emotional healing and deliverance, 2) determining God's calling in your life, and 3) interceding for your suitable companion before you meet.

Meanwhile, don't short-circuit the Father's plan by focusing on the partner before you're centered in God's purposes for you. Get moving on what stirs your passion. That's the trail where you're most likely to find a partner who values and shares it. It's not a formula; it's common sense. God is sovereign and can bring two people together any way He wants. But why not make it easier for Him—and in the long run, for yourself?

"It's really true," a woman once said to me after hearing this teaching. "When I met my husband Bob, he told me he was a realtor, but never talked much about that. He also mentioned that he played guitar and had a small music trio. We hit it off together, but I wasn't quite sure he was the one for me.

"Then one day he said his trio would be playing at a restaurant in town that night and asked if I'd like to come see him perform. I'll never forget sitting there at the table after dinner as he went over to the stage, picked up his guitar and sat down with the others. When he began to play, it was like someone deeper, even greater—a power that I hadn't seen before—came out of him. As I watched him get into his music, somehow

I knew I was seeing the real Bob at last—and that's when I fell in love with him."

Destiny is not about a paying job, but rather, about a growing person. (See "Making a Living, or Making a Life?" in *Sons of the Father*). Bob sold real estate, and was good at it. No doubt, his character came through as he did that. But when he played his music, something even more authentic to himself was revealed. The woman bonded with that because her heart was looking for the real Bob, even his most genuine passion.

It's worth declaring here that parenting most certainly qualifies as a calling—indeed, one of God's highest. For a man or woman who accepts it as such, parenting can reveal your true self far more deeply than a salaried profession.

WAGON TRAIN

Why is it so hard for men and women today to believe the simple, biblical truth that God has a purpose for you? And, even for those who do, why is it so hard to trust more in God's eternal purposes than the cry of the flesh?

Archetypically, the mother's job is to teach her child to feel loved and connected with other people in relationships; the father's job is to speak heritage and destiny, that is, to call the child forth into the world with a sense of life purpose. Both are necessary and equally important.

It's like the old wagon train of "Wild West" lore. The wagons set out westward after a destiny, on a straight line trajectory—a masculine image. But no one, no matter how focused and determined, can sustain that indefinitely.

At the end of the day's journey, therefore, the wagons draw together into a circle—a more feminine image. The wagon circle provides a sense of closeness and protection in the otherwise vast and dangerous plains. Within it, equipment is repaired, wounds are bandaged, harmonicas are played, stories are told, and relationships are re-enforced. Security, healing, and strengthening relationships are the hallmark of "circling the wagons."

The wagon train's mission, however, cannot be accomplished by remaining in a circle. In the morning, a man blows the bugle, and the circle opens again into a straight line, headed for its *destin*ation, as in *destiny*.

Certainly, both men and women may be able to perform both of these roles as needed. The lesson here lies in their complementing each other. Like a man and a woman, the straight line and the circle work together after the larger goal. The circle without the straight line beckons stagnation; the straight line without the circle leads to burnout. In either case, the mission is not accomplished.

Thus, unmothered children often have difficulty bonding emotionally to others. For women especially, their journey is harder, often without close female friendships to provide discerning input and uplifting support.

Fatherless children often have trouble focusing their lives productively. When dad is either physically or emotionally absent, that is, the prophesied curse of fatherlessness in Mal. 4:5,6 is loosed: his sons and daughters miss the essential preparation for life. Their gifts are not affirmed by the person anointed to call them forth into the world, so they lack confidence in their life purpose and the power to fulfill it.

That translates for sons into a generation of aimless men, uncertain about their place in the world. Under-bonded to Dad and over-bonded to Mom, they take refuge from the challenge of masculinity in femininity. Overwhelmed by shame, they trade truth for grace. Afraid to break away from Mom to focus on a wife, they become confused about their sexual identity. They wander from woman to woman, deriving a counterfeit masculinity in numerous sexual conquests—or they retreat from manhood into same-sex attraction.

DAUGHTER AND DAD

For daughters, not being affirmed by Dad often means seeking sex with many men to compensate for lost father-love and/or acceding to her husband's life because she has none of her own. All too often, she lacks self-worth and soon begins to feel trapped in her marriage, with little sense of her own desires and gifting to fulfill them. Soap opera fantasies feed on this lack of direction and identity via second-hand drama and sexuality, and can become an addictive diversion from reality.

On the other hand, when Dad affirms, encourages, and blesses his children's gifting and passion, they know they belong in this world, and want to make a difference with their lives. In fact, by the time they grow up and leave home, they look forward to focusing the talents and abilities Dad has affirmed.

Again, a sense of calling out into the world comes archetypically from Dad; without it, a child becomes ingrown and unfocused. The ability to sustain that calling comes from Mom; without that, a child can become alienated and unable to ask for help. In either case, without that balance, children grow up confused about their life purpose, and thereby, about choosing a mate with whom to fulfill it.

Father God has sent Jesus and thereby, released His Holy Spirit in this present age to heal these wounds, and thereby, reveal His calling upon your life and a suitable companion to fulfill it (see "Healing Emotional Wounds" in *Broken by Religion, Healed by God*).

Diagnosing an illness is the first step toward healing. It's never too late for a man or woman to ask God, "What did you have in mind when you created me?" This question beckons literally the greatest adventure of your life—and a deeper relationship with the One who designed it. What's more, it stirs the desire for a suitable companion to join you.

Even if you're already married, a couple can always ask the Father, "What did you have in mind when you brought us together?"

Trust that God has great plans for you as you receive the fullness of life Jesus came to give you.

BENEFIT OF SINGLENESS

If you're a single Christian, you have the benefit of fewer distractions from this task. Take responsibility now for discovering your purpose in life. Singleness offers time to deal with this issue clearly and directly. "When you're unmarried," as Paul declared,

> you're free to concentrate on simply pleasing the Master. Marriage involves you in all the nuts and bolts of domestic life and in wanting to please your spouse, leading to so many more demands on your attention. The time and energy that married people spend on caring for and

nurturing each other, the unmarried can spend
in becoming whole and holy instruments of
God. (1 Corinth. 7:32-35TMB).

Get on your face and cry out to your Father. Fast, pray, and ask Him what he had in mind when He created you. Listen to and honor what excites you to learn more. Step out, take a chance, go for the schooling, job, or opportunity where you can express your passion.

Give your Father God something to bless.

For most of us, your destiny is simply in your heart, and has been dormant there long before you dared to recognize it. Some people, like Moses, hear a clear, Ten Commandments voice out of the air. Most often, however, discovering your destiny is a process. Crying out amid its pains and celebrating its joys teach you relationship with the Father who designed it and thereby, prepare you for relationship with your partner.

In order to recognize what God is doing in you, clean your heart out so there's plenty of room there for Holy Spirit to show you. Ask Father God to search your heart, confess your sins to Him and to others you've sinned against. See a Christian counselor and get healing for past emotional wounds and deliverance from the spirits which would sabotage your holy calling. Listen for what stirs your passion and be bold to put yourself where He can clarify, focus, and bless it. Pray with trustworthy Christian friends for wisdom.

Above all, trust your Father. He wants to bring His Kingdom on earth as it is in heaven, and to clarify His vision in you so you can do your part to fulfill it. As He does, you're ready to ask Him for a suitable companion with whom to do it.

Again, this message is not just for singles. Many husbands and wives have never dedicated time and energy to ask God what He made them to do. Get on your knees side by side and ask Him. Commit to set out as fellow explorers on that new adventure together.

And be sure to book a hotel room out of town that night.

**

For our third date, I called Mary and said, "I'm going biking along the beach path near where I live and I'd like you to come with me."

A long pause on the other end unsettled me. *Did she not want to go with me? Or maybe she...*

"Yes…," she said finally, strangely hesitant. "Yes," she repeated, overwhelming my fearful thoughts with gathering conviction, "I'd really like to do that."

Months later when we were engaged, she brought up that conversation. "You know, so many men think they're being polite when they ask their date, 'What do you want to do?' But you said, 'This is where I'm going and I want you to come with me'. I've been waiting a long time for a man to say that to me."

> **Before the clothing comes off in marriage,
> the emotional covering must come off safely
> in order to enjoy each other without shame.**

4

Naked but not Ashamed

Learning to Trust

*Then the Lord God planted a garden in Eden, in the
East, and there he put the man that he had formed.
He made all kinds of beautiful trees grow there and
produce good fruit. Gen. 2:8*

THEY DON'T CALL IT PARADISE for nothing. Beautiful trees,
bountiful fruit. No sweat—literally. God makes everything grow, all for
the man Adam's own enjoyment. Doesn't get any better than this!

Or maybe it does. A whole lot better, in fact—at least, for those
whose hearts are real. Indeed, at the very beginning God declared that
Paradise was missing something essential, for which even the most
beautiful trees and tasty fruit can't compensate:

Then the Lord God said, "It is not good for the man to live alone" (Gen. 2:18).

Let me try to put this in modern English: When God downloads the Creation document into His "Earth" folder, a "Not Good" warning appears on the "Adam" file. Apparently, there's a chip in the masculine software such that if this program attempts to function independently, it will crash.

I experienced this years ago when I was courting Mary. On our second date, when I took her to Disneyland, we bought a pizza on the way home and brought it to my place. As we were going up the walkway to my doorstep, I paused to hand her the pizza so I could open the door.

I should note here that I'm not particularly gifted in the art of homemaking. In fact, the psychiatric Diagnostic and Statistical Manual includes a special category just for me. It's called "Domestically Challenged."

In any case, as I gestured her ahead hospitably, Mary stepped inside my living room—and stopped suddenly as if stunned in her tracks. Entering, I saw her jaw agape as her eyes swept my living room—where, I might further note, forms of the verb *to sweep* would not otherwise apply.

Her astonishment told me she was immensely impressed with my digs. Encouraged, I smiled. "Just go ahead and put the pizza on the table."

But the woman moved not. "Uh, well...," she stammered, "I mean..., where's the table?"

Helpfully, I pointed in the direction of my table—which unfortunately was obscured at the time by a number of file boxes and several excellent pool cues. Graciously, I led her around the pool table and cleared the boxes away. Gesturing toward the top of my dinner table, I pointed with unbridled humility to my place mat. There, a cherished but dated *Los Angeles Times* Sports page lay colorfully spotted with faded red ketchup, yellow mustard, and an artistic variety of dried condiments and leftovers.

Overwhelmed by my creativity, Mary drew up with measured breath. "Would you mind," she offered graciously, "if I maybe...tidied up just a bit?"

Bachelors are the last to discover this fact of life: Women are divinely ordained to "tidy up" a man's life—and not "just a bit." Two weeks after our wedding, I had a new kind of haircut and half my wardrobe benefited a nearby thrift store.

My initiation began dramatically when Mary reached to lift up my sporty place mat—and it ripped right between the goal post because, well, the other half stuck.

God was right. It's not good for the man to live alone.

It's just not sanitary.   *Ha, Ida*

HOPING AND SCOPING

Meanwhile, back in the Garden, Adam's moping around alone. Significantly, the Creator takes initiative Himself to rectify what's wrong. He doesn't say to the man, "You're seriously in need of something that your destiny requires. So go find out what that is and get it!" Young singles in my Southern California beach town church used to call it "hoping and scoping."

Rather, the Father Himself provides:

I will make a suitable companion to help him (Gen. 2:18b).

Note the key word here, *suitable*—that is, someone who suits or fits you, who complements your life, who adds what you don't have in order literally to full-fill God's plan for you. As noted in the last chapter, a marriage after God's purposes begins not with shared desire, but rather, with shared destiny.

You can't separate sexuality from life purpose.

Clearly, you can't know your purpose apart from the Creator God who designed it. This spiritual connection undergirds sexual attraction. Sexual desire, that is, focuses on your partner. But its fulfillment is defined by God's purpose for your life together.

> *So he took some soil from the ground and formed all the animals and all the birds. Then he brought them to the man to see what he would name them; and that is how they all got their names* (Gen. 2:19).

Hold on. What's all this talk about animals? Let's cut to the chase: I thought we were going for the suitable companion?

In fact, the Father Himself knows the animals are not the headliner act, but the opener. Apparently, He has a larger agenda here—a process, a more suitable time line for His purposes:

> So the man named all the birds and all the
> animals...

Imagine Adam, life-breathed in the Garden, admiring the beautiful trees, enjoying the tasty fruit day after day after day...after day.

Eventually, the Father checks in. "How's everything going, son? Do you like the trees and fruit I've provided for you?"

"They're great, Father," we can imagine Adam's responding—and then hesitating. "Well, actually..., to be honest, the trees are all fine, but have you got something that maybe moves, you know, that can come along with me where I go?"

"No problem, son," the Father declares, beckoning the animals. "Have I got a treat for you! Look at all these great companions. You'll have the time of your life riding this horse. Wait 'til you play with this dog—a man's best friend! And how about some fish to catch, some birds and deer to hunt—animals everywhere, all kinds, moving around just like you!"

At that, Adam cheers up. In fact, he rides his horse, plays with his dog, and goes fishing. And rides his horse, plays with his dog, goes fishing. And rides his horse...until before long, he's bored yet again and moping around the garden.

LIKE ME

The Father re-visits to test Adam's readiness. "So how do you like my animals, son?"

"Well, Father, they're all great. But..."

"But what, son?" the Father urges.

"Now, I don't want to sound ungrateful. I mean, like me the dog and all the others have two holes in their faces for air, two eyes, two ears, and four limbs. They move around like I asked for. At least, during the day. But I've noticed that at night they all go off together by themselves, two by two."

The man hesitates, uncertain but determined.

With a hint of anticipation, the Father draws closer. "What do you mean, son? Is something…*missing*, maybe?"

"Yes, Father—that's it!" Adam exclaims. "It's like an emptiness or hunger—so deep that nothing else in the world satisfies it. It's strange, like something inside me, but at the same time out there that I want. I don't know what it is. I don't even…have a name for it."

…but not one of them was a suitable companion to help him (Gen. 2:20).

Struggling, Adam pushes ahead. "I guess I want something…more. I mean, have you got anything…that's more…."

A hush falls upon the Garden as creation itself holds its breath.

"More…what, son?"

"Well, more…like…like *me*, Father?"

Now is The Time.

Here a last is the humble, heartfelt openness in His son that the Father's been waiting for. For Adam/humankind, it's the moment of holy awareness, of readiness for life—The Moment, in fact, on which history not only turns, but where history itself begins.

Not until all of creation has been found good yet lacking, is the man ready to seek the very best. If your ball games and work and cars and buddies and hunting trips are all you need, my brother, go ahead. Be strong and independent, and enjoy yourself. It's good.

But until you face that emptiness in your heart, until you can confess that it's not good to live alone, that you're not whole and fully yourself when you're without a suitable companion—you're not ready for the Best.

When you *are* ready, however, so is the Father:

> *Then the Lord God made the man fall into a deep sleep, and while he was sleeping, He took out one of the man's ribs and closed up the flesh* (Gen. 2:21).

OK, wait another minute. First the animals, and now we're going to sleep? Where's the woman? I thought this was the Big Moment to get turned on!

GENERAL ANAESTHESIA

Once again, the man must submit to the Father's sequence. Adam's "sleep" is the general anesthesia before the operation. His experiences in the world, that is, have wounded and infected him. You can't just leap after the woman without first going under the Surgeon's knife for healing—or you'll both end up not only infected, but contagious.

The Father has a plan for His son and daughter, and you need to get ready to recognize and fulfill it. That means to seek forgiveness for times you've turned away from God, healing for your childhood wounds, and deliverance from how the enemy has taken advantage of your brokenness.

And let's face it: we men are often as if asleep in a relationship, unaware of the deeper consequences it beckons.

When Mary and I had been married about a year, she asked me a surprising question one morning over breakfast: "Don't you think it's time we talked about starting a family?"

Startled, I looked up from my scrambled eggs and stared ahead. "Uh, well,…" I offered, pausing uncertain. Sure, at 45 I'd thought about having kids someday—but was otherwise content to leave the issue in my "Later" file. As Mary sat there waiting for my response, a rising uneasiness urged me to retreat—but I checked it. In fact, I knew I needed to move boldly to overcome it. The best defense, after all, is a good offense.

"Well, sure," I managed, gathering myself and leaping ahead. "This is a great time to talk about starting a family. In fact, why don't we just think about some names—you know, like boys' and girls' names?"

"You mean like, for our children?" Mary said, leaning forward with more than a hint of determination. "I think that's a great idea!" Smiling quickly, she reached to pick up her prayer journal on the table. "Actually, I just happen to have a few names right here."

"You have names…for our children?" I asked, puzzled. "I mean, like, already?"

"Well, yes—just a few," Mary noted very casually, opening her journal to an earlier page and beckoning me to look.

In fact, she did have names for our children. Written down, right there on the page where the word "Disneyland" appeared several times. Confused, I noticed the day and month at the top: It was just after our second date!

The man thought they were just playing with Mickey Mouse. The woman was planning their future.

While he was sleeping....

Indeed.

HOLY OPERATION

For so the holy operation begins.

> *...he took out one of the man's rib and closed up the flesh. He formed a woman out of the rib and brought her to him* (Gen. 2:22).

The Father's greatest desire is to enjoy mutual relationship with his creature Adam. Building that relationship with Him is based on integrating our lives with His purposes. And so, for construction material he uses none other than parts of the man himself.

That means you need to sacrifice a part of yourself to get that relationship.

It's not always easy. Often, a man and a woman don't see things alike. "If you're both the same, one of you is unnecessary," as another has said. In order to grow together toward your destiny, that is, words like communication, compromise, surrender, forgiveness, humility, and trust must be given credibility in your heart.

Even so, we can imagine the excitement in heaven when God first brings Eve to Adam.

"It's time!" the Father calls out. "Wake up, son! Come out of your bachelor stupor. Open your eyes to the larger picture of what I'm doing in your life. You thought hunting with that dog, riding the horse, and fishing were something? Wait 'til you see what I have for you now!"

Adam yawns, rubs his eyes, sits up, and looks.

And awakes with a start! Wholly alert at last, in wonder he reaches out to touch the woman—and a holy recognition bursts forth:

> *Then the man said, "At last! Here is one of my own kind—bone taken from my bone and flesh taken from my flesh. 'Woman' is her name, because she was taken out of man.*

For this reason, a man will leave his father
and mother and be united to his wife and they will
become one flesh (Gen. 2:23,24NIV)

"At last"—after much longing and preparation—the man has a companion truly suitable. She who was literally a part of himself is therefore now what he lacks in order to be whole—that is, the missing complement to himself, even to his destiny.

FOR THIS REASON

Clearly, the words "united" and "one flesh" refer to sexual intercourse. Here, in fact, lies the root of sexual desire as defined by the very One who created it. But what does the simple but key phrase "for this reason" mean? Indeed, for *what* reason do a man and woman desire each other?

To recap: The name Adam means "humankind" in Hebrew. In the Beginning, that is, all of humanity was comprised by one single body. But that was not good because the Father wants relationship with His children, and you can't learn relationship without relating to an "other." So God separates humankind into two distinct beings, man and woman.

The purpose of gender difference, therefore, is to provide a context in which partners can grow in relationship with Father God and be shaped to further His created purpose for them. The differences, in fact, are the proverbial grain of sand in the oyster, the holy irritant which forces the couple to the feet of Jesus for His shaping—and the often abrasive process of "polishing."

Clearly, same-gender sexual relationships cannot reflect the image of God, which is male and female, nor the nature of the Creator, because they're not configured to create new life together.

Furthermore, couples who engage in sex apart from God's covenant in marriage are more vulnerable to the father of Lies and his destructive purposes. Apart from a sense of destiny inherent to suitable companions, the calling and attraction can easily be reduced to mere legal categories like "mutual consent." Ultimately, sex apart from surrender to the God who created it distracts from His purpose and at worst, sabotages it.

Even married couples, of course, can struggle to reach the harmony God intends for them. We live in a fallen world, and until Jesus returns, that fallen-ness lives in us. None of us is perfectly surrendered to God. All growing couples will fight at times. The question is not whether a man and woman will fight, but to whom will they turn when they do?

A couple surrendered to Jesus learn to let their conflicts drive them first, out of their own embrace; second, into the arms of God, and last but not least, back into each other's arms for His restoration. It's a humbling, often frustrating and painful process. But if you're going to serve God in this broken world, you've got to give Him every chance to reveal and overcome its brokenness in you.

Thus—as we'll see in Chapter 15, "Never Waste a Good Fight"— the pain of conflict which would drive a couple apart instead becomes an avenue for deeper relationship with both God and each other. That's the miracle of redemption. It's how Father God's embrace seizes victory from the enemy's grasp.

"You don't know that Jesus is all you need," as wisely said, "until Jesus is all you have." Couples seasoned by both fear and faith know this, because they have experienced it together (see Hebrews 5:13,14).

Meanwhile, back in the Garden, a major a problem remains. Just because God has made two separate people doesn't guarantee that they'll want to come back together and relate. They could just walk off in different directions and never re-connect. Nor would humanity propagate itself.

HOLY MEMORY

With divine genius, the Father therefore places within each partner a holy memory chip in both the masculine and feminine software, a defining desire in their very bodies to go back to the one-ness that was Adam-in-the-Beginning, before the distinction of Eve. That restored one-ness, in fact, will be the avenue by which new life itself is created.

Here at last, is the root origin of sexual attraction.

We want to return, that is, to the wholeness from whence we came. Of all human experiences, sexual intercourse most graphically re-connects the two as one and reminds them of that perfect place of origin. Sexual attraction beckons the closest thing to Paradise on earth.

In God's plan, sex is a marvelous blessing. Lest we allow that blessing to pre-empt its qualifications, however, we must heed its key foundation: "a man shall leave his mother and father." Both the man and the woman, that is, were once boy and girl, each growing up in a family, which shaped their expectations of marriage.

The Story says you must "leave father and mother" in order to form the new family God has prepared for you. It's simple—but any married couple knows it's not easy. Images of "how Mom and Dad did it" are branded on your hard drive; saying Goodbye is not easy. The worldly security of living emotionally like your parents must be surrendered to Father God for His re-shaping. That means overcoming the fear and shame which attends leaving them. Plenty of self-honesty, mutual understanding, and loving patience is required.

In fact, the first man every woman loves is her daddy. The character of that relationship imprints upon her heart and defines for her what it's like to love a man. The words "family" and "familiar" share the same root. When she grows into womanhood, therefore, the woman will naturally seek to replicate with her mate the *familiar* feelings she most often felt in her girlhood *family* around Dad—for better or worse.

If Dad were kind, thoughtful, loving, protective, providing, and able to set boundaries without shaming, she learns to feel safe, protected, loved, and respected with a man. She'll naturally look for those *family*-iar qualities in a mate.

ATTRACTED TO FAMILIAR

On the other hand, if Dad were shaming, punishing, disengaged, absent and/or abusive, she learns to feel denigrated, insecure, and afraid with a man. As a woman she'll be drawn to a man who shares those *familiar* character traits and makes her feel similarly negative about herself—no matter how damaging to her feminine soul.

Because this dynamic is so deeply linked to Dad, it feels *familiar*— and therefore, becomes confused with love (see "Fathers and Daughters" in *Healing the Masculine Soul*). That's why women who suffered abuse from their fathers often marry abusive husbands, and why women who grew up without a father are drawn to men who are often emotionally distant or physically away from home.

Similarly, the first woman every man loves is his mother. She defines for him what it's like to love a woman. If she's caring, encouraging, comforting, and able to set healthy boundaries, as a man he'll be drawn to a woman like that. If she's shaming, distant, irritable, and possessive, he'll grow up feeling unloved and insecure with a woman. He'll misinterpret those negative traits as a woman's love and seek a "familiar" wife who makes him feel similarly unloved, insecure, and pre-empted, as when he was a boy with Mom.

Such family dynamics are organic and deeply ingrown. Even if your spouse does not manifest your opposite-sex parent's dysfunction, you're easily tempted to prompt it in him/her, that is, to nudge the other into the image of that parent and re-create the false but familiar "comfort" in your conflicted childhood family. If the marriage partners don't face this fact, subconsciously the woman will treat her husband as her mom treated her dad; the man will treat his wife as his father treated his mother—for better or worse.

The most ancient of Scriptures anticipates this confusion, and essentially warns men and women to deal with their childhood family wounds—that is, to "leave father and mother"—before attempting to bond emotionally and sexually with a mate.

The overwhelming task here is to "honor your father and mother," as an adult, but not to worship them, as a child (Exod. 20:12). The innate parent-child bond is literally so natural, however, that it requires *supernatural* power to overcome and re-define.

Unfortunately, too many couples marry without ever having faced and questioned their misconceived childhood sense of love. It feels familiar, which compels you unconsciously to expect and even replicate it. Eventually, you bring your childhood dysfunction into your marriage, unto yet another generation in your children, who witness it.

Thus, in order to recreate their childhood sense of family, a wife tries to make her husband into her father's image and a man tries to make his wife into his mother's image. The two of you remain emotionally as children. Nobody grows up and you sabotage God's plan for you as adults.

It's all a charade, designed to avoid the pain and fear of developing a healthy, mature relationship with a marriage partner—and of trusting God to work with you in that struggle. And yet such efforts to avoid pain only create more wounding and distance.

Nor does sexual desire flow freely.

MARITAL DISCORD

As any marriage counselor knows, this natural urge to remain within the emotional/spiritual force-field of your parents is the root of most marital discord. Until you confess your natural fears of leaving Mom and Dad, and seek God for His unique, adult purposes for you, your marriage bond is not complete and remains unfulfilled. That's precisely because your vision is co-opted by your childhood images, which distract you from God's purposes for you as adults.

Effective marriage counseling, especially related to a vital sexuality, doesn't get down to business until each partner is asked, "How was your relationship with your opposite sex parent?" (see "Cutting the Cord: A Second Postpartum" in *Sons of the Father* and "Fathers and Daughters" in *Healing the Masculine Soul*).

Meanwhile, back in the Garden, our primal Story ends on a profound word of hope. In fact, the final, crowning verse jars us out of our accumulated shame to a place of wonder, of primal trust:

The man and woman were both naked, but
they were not ashamed (Gen. 2:25).

While the word *naked* here certainly refers to uncovered bodies, it hints at a prior, even more fundamental uncovering of hearts.

Before meeting Mary, my childhood and earlier relationships with women included much wounding by both parties. I needed to forgive those who had wounded me, seek forgiveness for my wounding them, and receive emotional healing and deliverance to keep my heart open for a future wife.

Soon after Mary and I met, my heart began opening to her beyond any depth I had previously allowed. I looked forward to seeing her, thought about her often, felt strong doing good things for her, appreciated her love, was excited to be with her, enjoyed our common interests, and could easily see us growing together in the future. After just three months together, it was clear to us and to all credible witnesses that this was the marriage God had prepared for us.

Wonderful as all this felt, however, the vulnerability which sponsored it stirred deep fears within me which my earlier relationship wounds, unto my childhood, had led me to cover up. I knew if I dawdled, my fears could define us and the enemy would steal it all. I asked Mary to marry me.

Soon after we were engaged, the enemy roared in like a flood. Sheets of cold darkness seized my body, at times almost paralyzing me.

Now, at last, I had no choice; it was time to meet the enemy head-on and trust Jesus to help me face and overcome my deepest fears. Otherwise, I knew my heart would remain closed and cowed, and I would miss out on the fulfilling marriage and future which I had worked and prayed for so long.

I tried hard. With renewed hope, I sought out more prayer partners, went to more healing conferences, fasted, cast more demons out of me, got counseling, cried out to the Father, prayed, prayed, and prayed some more.

All necessary, but not sufficient. The fears continued.

In my spiritual warfare ministry, I've always taught that the flak is thickest when you're over the target, that the intensity of the battle is proportionate to the significance of the victory. I knew that God had called Mary and me together, that this at times overwhelming battle for my heart reflected His momentous plans for us—which required that victory. Wanting badly to prove I was man enough to take responsibility for my own healing and press ahead after it, I withheld as much of my struggle from Mary as possible.

ENEMY'S TRUMP CARD

Persevering, I nevertheless was cut to the core when the enemy produced a trump card in my mind that played masterfully upon my pride, isolation, and distrust. I began to think I had wimped out, that my fears only confirmed I was not man enough—neither for Mary nor for my role in the destiny God had set for us. Certainly, this thought concluded, Mary did not deserve a coward for a husband.

I became so oppressed by this thought that I knew I had to confess my fears to Mary—fully expecting her to break off the engagement. As if to confirm my self-judgment, I waited until the last minute—the day, in fact, when we had scheduled to pick up our wedding rings at the jeweler's downtown Los Angeles.

I remember walking deliberately up to her apartment door, taking a deep breath and bracing myself to do what a man must do. I was late, and when I knocked, Mary opened the door immediately to step out.

"I...I need to talk to you about something," I managed quickly, gesturing for her to wait.

"That's fine," Mary offered. "But we're late, so can you just talk to me in the car on the way?"

"Not... really," I replied—knowing that what I had to say would cancel any need for the jeweler. "Could we maybe...just go inside together for a minute?"

Uncertain, Mary paused. "Well, OK. If it's just for a minute."

Together, we stepped into her apartment and I sat down opposite her near the door, to save energy when she kicked me out. After an uncomfortable moment, I began.

"There's...something we need...to talk about," I began. And then, I knew it was no use.

"Listen," I burst out, "I'm scared. I mean, I love you and you're better than anything I could've asked for and I want to marry you. I don't want to be scared, but I've tried everything I know to do but I just can't get over it."

Mary hesitated, then looked quickly at her watch.

Here it comes, I thought—steeling myself for the blow.

"Yes, I'm scared, too," she noted. "Getting married is the biggest decision we'll ever make after giving our lives to the Lord. There's no absolute guarantee everything will work out the way we want."

I drew up, confused.

"So what is it you want to talk about?" she asked matter-of-factly. "It's getting late."

I sat dumbfounded. "You..., I mean, you're scared, too?"

"Yes, of course," she declared. "All we really have is Jesus and each other—but we have faith He's with us in this."

I leapt to embrace her. Naked, I was—but no longer ashamed.

"Hey, we'll be late for the jeweler's!" I exclaimed after a moment. "Let's get going!"

Certainly, deeper healing lay ahead for both of us as we grew together. But the freedom to be real with one another in that critical moment laid the foundation for the growing.

Some time later, before the wedding, I confessed to Mary that I had thought she would stop loving me and break off our relationship when I exposed my fear to her.

"Actually," she declared, "When you told me you were scared, I loved you more."

"*More?*" I exclaimed, puzzled. "How could you love me *more*, knowing I was weak like that?"

Mary smiled thoughtfully. "You trusted me," she said simply. "I've waited a long time for that in a man."

THREE KINDS OF MEN

Later, Mary and I spoke at a singles conference together and I was startled when she addressed the women. "In a relationship, there are three kinds of men," she declared. "All men are scared when it comes to commitment.

"The first kind of man is scared and runs away. He's saved you a lot of trouble. Count yourself blessed and move on.

"The second kind of man is scared and dumps his shame on you. He criticizes you and drives you to reject him, so he doesn't have to be the bad guy and leave. This kind of relationship is the very worst."

Turning to me, Mary smiled graciously. "The third kind of man is scared, and says so. He works on his fears and presses through them to commit. That's integrity and strength. That's the man you're looking for."

Talk about redemption.

Thank you, Father!

Prepare for physical union by developing emotional trust. Let God teach you. Ultimately, it's not about trusting each other, but trusting the Father—so deeply that whatever happens, you know He'll use it to draw you closer to Him and His purposes.

That's what the engagement period is for. But if you're married and didn't know all this back then, you can still commit together to trust God more deeply—that is, even now to surrender to each other more openly and communicate more vulnerably.

Sure, naked bodies are a significant part of the marriage covenant. But before the material covering comes off, the emotional covering must be safely removed if the bodies are to respond joyfully, without shame. Too many couples get it backwards, jumping into sex, assuming that will catapult them into intimacy—and wondering later why the sex fades when conflicts inevitably arise.

Trusting God and learning to know each other is the best foreplay. Respect your heart and get real with each other. Give your Father a chance to make it happen.

> The impulse to modesty is rooted in our human sin-nature. It can't be overridden without beckoning the shame of that sin-nature and wounding your heart.

5

Anatomy of a Blush

The Genesis of Modesty

The man and his wife were both naked, and they were not ashamed. Gen. 2:25RSV

As soon as they had eaten (the forbidden fruit), they were given understanding and realized that they were naked; so they sewed fig leaves together and covered themselves. Gen. 3:7

FROM OUR VERY GENESIS AS A SPECIES, a pervasive shame hovers over sexuality and abides to blackmail us into secrecy and isolation. But what makes us associate sexual desire and exposure with shame? Is it all just an imposed cultural taboo or a fabricated religious guilt trip?

Or, indeed, could sexual desire in fact reflect a deeper reality rooted in unrectifiable wrongdoing?

Others have made the essential distinction between guilt, which is about something you've done, and shame, which is about who you are. The former can be rectified by making amends; the latter, by no human effort. This view begs the larger question: Is there something fundamentally, even intrinsically flawed, broken, or defective in our human nature itself which thereby stirs shame, and is related to sexuality?

The Bible offers a helpful clue to this mystery at the very outset of human life in the idyllic Garden of Eden story. In the beginning, that is, Adam and Eve lived wholly innocent before God, untainted by any inclination to rebel or turn away from Him. This altogether childlike freedom and trust allowed the first man and woman to be "naked *but not ashamed*" together (Gen. 2:25, italics mine).

Being naked means your gender is manifestly clear. When Adam and Eve covered their sexual parts as a concession to shame, this primary consequence of the Fall means a less manifest gender identity, and in that sense, allows for gender confusion.

But what if from creation itself your manhood or your womanhood were unapologetically clear as well—with no need for justification, desperation to prove, or compulsion to comply with either politically correct ideology or religiously correct morality? Indeed, what if from its very genesis sexual attraction is simply "good"—as God declared His creation (Gen. 1:25)?

If so, how did we forget or lose this innocence and instead feel shameful about our sexuality? Indeed, can this loss be remedied?

ORDAINED INNOCENCE

In the Creation story, the power of evil enters to tempt the man and woman away from the Father—whose love has ordained their innocence to protect them from just such an attack. In the form of a snake, the evil one slanders God rather as a jealous tyrant who enforces their innocence to keep them ignorant and thereby subservient.

"Did God really tell you not to eat fruit from any tree in the garden?" the snake scoffs to Eve:

"We may eat the fruit of any tree in the garden," the woman answered, "except the tree in the middle of it. God told us not to eat the fruit of that tree or even touch it; if we do, we will die."

The snake replied, "That's not true; you will not die. God said that because he knows that when you eat it, you will be like God and know what is good and what is bad." (Gen. 3:2-5)

Lured by the snake's promise of untasted, forbidden freedom, Eve not only eats the fruit, but draws Adam into the lie by sharing it with him as well. The consequences of their trusting the snake over God are immediate and upending—and focus first on their sexuality:

As soon as they had eaten it, they were given understanding and *realized they were naked*; so they sewed fig leaves together and covered themselves. (Gen. 3:7 italics mine)

Significantly, the evidence of their distrusting God manifests in their sexuality. Here lies the genesis not only of shame itself, but its root connection to sexuality.

Reflecting that shame with their leaf coverings, the man and woman try to hide when the Father later calls out to Adam, "Where are you?"

(Adam) answered, "I heard you in the garden; I was afraid and hid from you *because I was naked*."

"Who told you that *you were naked*?" God asked. "Did you eat the fruit that I told you not to eat?" (Gen. 3:10,11, italics mine).

ORGANIC BOUNDARY

The impulse to modesty is the organic boundary of shame, rooted in our archetypal memory of lost innocence. The natural balk at exposing yourself, therefore, is a holy reminder of your inborn sin nature and your inability to overcome it in your own strength. When God's boundaries challenge our desires, modesty marks a fork in the road of faith—after which you either distrust God and "do it my way" or trust that doing it His way will fulfill His larger, created purposes for you.

From a biblical perspective, the impulse to modesty is intrinsic to our human sin-nature, an inborn response to cover its exposure and not simply imposed extrinsically by culture or religion. As such, it cannot be overridden without prompting that sin-nature and wounding the human heart.

Today's widespread sexual exposure, urged by popular media, therefore comes at a severe cost—especially to the hearts of women, who largely bear its focus. To push yourself beyond what your heart tells you is shameful and wounding, requires you to disengage from reality. Ultimately, you must desensitize, even deny and disrespect your core identity as a man or woman.

The world, meanwhile, tells a woman that exposing herself is courageous. "Ex-model, 62, nearly bares all in interview," headlined a recent *Huffington Post* article. "It had been decades since Jacky disrobed in front of a camera until this brave interview."[11] What the world esteems in a woman as "brave," however, Father God sees as a pathetic attempt to dispel shame by your own efforts—something you can't do, and in fact, which Jesus has already done. Often, it's a misguided longing for affirmation—which makes the Father grieve for His daughter's wounded heart and inability to integrate His defining respect for her.

"Government, like dress, is a badge of lost innocence," as American revolutionary Thomas Paine wrote. Similarly, we might say that modesty testifies to our loss of innocence in Eden. Inasmuch as Jesus came to overcome our sin nature and restore our innocence before God, the impulse to modesty stirs at the boundary between childlike openness and weathered caution. In that sense, it reflects our distance from Father God and will remain as an organic human impulse until Jesus returns to restore us wholly to Him. Yes, Jesus told His followers to be "innocent as doves." But in the same breath he urged that we be "wise as a serpent" (Matt. 10:16).

INTRINSIC MODESTY

In fact, Adam and Eve's fig leaves say that modesty is as intrinsic to human nature as sin—that is, our innate human propensity to turn away from God. It can only be denied precisely insofar as we deny our sin nature—and thereby, our need to be saved from it. Such ignorance is not bliss, but rather, arrogant presumption which cuts you off from God and His purposes in your life.

Immodesty thereby reflects a refusal to face our fallen human condition. It bears shame because it reminds of our separation from Father God, now as then—and consequent inability on our own to measure up to His calling. Anyone who has, for example, watched pornography, committed adultery, or fornicated knows that separation—and the subsequent denial required to suppress it. The world, in fact, literally banks on it via the dramatic tension such acts stir in R-rated films.

Indeed, only within the holy covenant of marriage, covered by God's *super*natural power and grace, is the shame of nakedness truly overcome. Only within that eternal commitment to their Creator and each other, do a man and woman enjoy the freedom to uncover themselves and engage without fear in the physical act which beckons creation.

The world's notion of unrestrained sex or "free love" is therefore false and destructive not because it flies in the face of morality, but because it counterfeits the authentic freedom God has given us in Jesus—not a freedom *from* restrictions, but a freedom *to* fulfillment. Through the grace of Jesus, that is, our self-centered sin nature is overcome. You can cry out to Him in its grip, receive His mercy and the grace to get on with your divine destiny.

Cleansed and empowered, a husband and wife can give and receive. They can enjoy the genuine trust and intimacy together which flows only under the Father's protection and blessing.

Because sexual attraction ultimately lies beyond our natural ability to control, it stirs deep fear of condemnation and rejection. We therefore seek desperately to deny and pre-empt our vulnerability to its power.

The logical extreme of such deliberate denial is nudism, a graphic human attempt to seize innocence and override the danger/shame signal of modesty. In an effort to overcome our fallen nature apart from God, nudism denies both our innate longing for union with God and each other, and our need for saving power to fulfill it as intended. Ironically, the presumption inherent to nudism is thereby the same as to religion, namely, to overcome by human power the shame which can only be overcome by God—Who in fact has done so in Jesus.

NUDISM AND RELIGION

Get ready for supreme irony: Nudism and religion are bedfellows, both animated by the same spirit of pride.

While relatively few would practice outright nudism, a major thrust of "modern" Western culture is arrogantly to flirt with it much as a "daredevil" flirts with death. Among men, for example, the daredevil strives by entertaining danger to prove he's not subject to its power and can maintain his own strength and dignity even in the face of death. Similarly, women's magazines often refer to a revealing dress as "daring"— that is, insofar as it suggests her nakedness and thereby risks the primal "danger" of shame.

From spandex to bikinis, our secularized culture peddles the literally dare-devil fantasy that no human impulse lies beyond our ability to control and indulge with impunity. A people desperate to overcome their shame buy it wholesale.

Nudism, as the logical extension of suggestive clothing, proclaims to a shame-filled culture, "We're not subject to the power of the world and can save ourselves from its threat to define and restrict us!"

Christians, meanwhile, believe that Jesus will someday return to restore complete and authentic innocence as in Eden, that is, before God and not simply before one another. Until then, we'll be stirred to cover our sexual parts. Insofar as we fail to respect that impulse, we'll give rein to our sin-nature and wound our hearts.

The natural balk at exposing your body, therefore, is a yellow warning light in your heart which means, "The enemy of the God who created sexuality is present to subvert His intention, and you don't have the power to protect yourself from that."

Significantly, Adam and Eve's eating from the Tree of the Knowledge of Good and Evil and subsequent loss of innocence stirs bodily covering. Sexual "modesty" therefore reflects primarily not cultural taboo or moral sensibility, but rather an organic vulnerability which needs protection— without which our hearts will be violated and our created purpose compromised.

Adam and Eve's fig leaves demonstrate that sexuality focuses the distinction between good and evil, and thereby hosts the battle therein. Insofar as God made humanity "male and female" in His image, the enemy thereby focuses on distorting God's image by distorting sexuality.

REMEDIAL ACTION

Conceivably, exposure to the knowledge of good and evil could have led Adam and Eve to a variety of remedial action. They could have covered their mouths in order not to betray themselves through speech, bound their feet to prevent ready access to the forbidden fruit, or otherwise inflicted self-punishment.

But they covered their genitals.

Why?

Certainly, wrongdoing can have physical effects. Caught with a hand in the cookie jar, a child feels shame—and responds physically: an urge to withdraw amid increased heartbeat, face flushed, head drooping, and shoulders bent in fear. The very scientific credibility of a lie detector depends upon this phenomenon. Similarly, where shame has not been surrendered to Jesus and overcome by the grace of God in His marriage covenant, sexual exposure stirs a blush.

Even when married, Christian partners can blush together at times. That hints not only at primal shame, but the redeeming power of God to deliver them into overwhelming grace. We're not saved by marriage; we're saved by Jesus. Until He returns, our human nature will not be fully redeemed. Yet between husband and wife, a blush can remind them not just of their shame, but indeed, of the far greater Power Who covers it by attending their sexual relationship.

Nevertheless, major questions remain. Why, from the very genesis of our creation, do the defining sexual parts of Adam and Eve draw the immediate bodily effects of their shame from disobeying God? Indeed, what does this connection between shame and sexuality imply for our relationships as men and women?

The Story says that our Original distrust of the Father and its consequent shame became situated in our sexuality. Since our humiliating exit from the Garden, we wonder unto today: How, amid a flood of sexual images in popular media, can we redeem and re-discover the authentic roots of sexual attraction, discern its created purpose, and enjoy its intended fulfillment?

Before attempting to answer this question, we need to examine the other side of the coin, namely, modesty in men.

Yes, you read that correctly: modesty in men.

> I no longer consider myself a liberated
> male—just one who struggles to submit to
> women in their competence and to God in
> His.

6

The Modest Male

Men and Boundaries

*Yes, my children, remain in union with (Christ),
so that when he appears we may be full of courage
and need not hide in shame from him on the Day he
comes.* 1 John 2:28

I'VE ALWAYS CONSIDERED MYSELF a liberated male—at least,
until my cherished self-image was fearfully upended at a doctor's office.

It all started with a urinary tract infection. For a while, I ignored it
with customary bravado, but soon the pain became severe, and I knew I
needed to get help.

Even then, I balked. Urinary tract inspection, I knew from
memorable experience, requires a prostate exam—which, as every

man knows, can not only be excruciatingly painful, but is altogether unparalleled for its indignity.

Resolutely, I asked a doctor friend to recommend an urologist, whom I promptly called. The secretary informed me that he was on vacation and offered to schedule me instead with another doctor on the staff, a "Dr. Paul." Anxious for relief, I agreed.

Even as I struggled to put the impending ordeal out of my mind, I congratulated myself later as I strode into the medical building for my appointment. At least, I had sought help for my problem and not resisted out of macho pride.

Approaching the elevator doors pumped with self-confidence, I turned quickly to the glassed-in "Doctors" index on the wall to double-check that I was in the right place. I glanced toward the end, under the "P"s, and caught the surname *Paul* just as the elevator doors opened before me. Reassured, I was about to turn and enter when the full listing leapt out at me: "Paul, M.D., Dr. Joy."

"*Dr. Joy*"?

I stood frozen, my eyes riveted to the index. In that moment, I was aware of several other persons stepping around me to enter the waiting elevator.

"Are you getting on?" a voice asked from within.

With a start, I turned to see the others standing puzzled before me in the open elevator.

"Uh, well…," I muttered quickly, hesitating as the large steel doors shuddered before me. "I mean…well, I guess not," I said. "No…thank you."

The doors swooshed shut and I stood there alone, facing the polished steel.

WOMAN UROLOGIST

Catching myself, I looked around and was relieved to see that no one was watching me. Quickly, I crossed the lobby to a corner chair and sat down as thoughts and feelings warred within me.

"Joy Paul"…. *A woman urologist?* I exclaimed silently. *The prostate exam is bad enough as it is!*

Immediately, it occurred to me that I could simply leave right then, call the secretary later, and explain that I had just decided to wait until the original doctor returned from his vacation.

A flush of embarrassment swept over me. Why was I so upset? Certainly, I had campaigned for women's rights since my college activist days in the sixties, and had encouraged many women in their own professions even as their incomes often outpaced mine. I had learned from women professors, work associates, and counselors, having discussed many "embarrassing" things with the latter.

What's more, most women have male gynecologists—until relatively recently with no choice for a female doctor. For the first time I wondered how women felt about that.

At once it struck me: Maybe I didn't really need medical treatment after all.

But no, there was the pain again.

In that moment, a sensation of hopelessness filled me. Desperately, I prayed. *God, help me*, I sighed in dismay. *I didn't know I had this kind of fear in me. I don't want it, so give me the courage to go ahead.*

I sat waiting for God to answer my prayer, but sensed nothing but my fear. Realizing I had no logical defense, I stood up, gathered myself, and resolutely stepped up to the elevator. With a deep breath, I reached out and pushed the upward arrow.

Moments later, at the doctors' counter, I checked in. Soon afterward, the receptionist welcomed me, led me to the examining room, and handed me a standard hospital gown.

"Please remove your clothes and put this on," she instructed pleasantly. "The doctor will be with you in a moment."

"Uh, sure," I mumbled unpleasantly, forcing a quick smile in return as she left and closed the door behind her.

I'd worn hospital gowns plenty of other times at appointments, but somehow this one seemed not only open at the back, but not very closed in front and shorter than the others. Minutes later—disrobed completely and re-robed minimally—I sat gingerly atop the cold table.

LITTLE COMFORT

Glancing nervously around the room, I found little comfort in the colorful uro-genital tract sketches surrounding me on the walls. Quickly, I drew up and decided to rehearse in my mind a casual tone of voice for the doctor, in which I would explain my problem to her. "Hi, Doctor Paul!" I chirped under my breath. "How's everything go—"

The chick-click of the doorknob's turning silenced my voice, but amplified my heartbeat.

Too late.

Sucking in a deep breath, I pasted a smile on my face and fixed my eye on the door.

To my utter astonishment, in stepped a man, dark skinned in white shirt and tie. "Hello," he offered amiably in a distinct Indian accent, extending his hand. "I'm Doctor Joy Paul."

Amid an angelic chorus of praise—or so it seemed—a deep, deep sigh escaped my lips. Heedless of my flailing gown, I leapt up to seize his hand and, to his surprise, pumped it enthusiastically.

I never inquired whether Joy is a male name in India, or perhaps, an Anglicized version of some other Indian name. I can only confess that the indignity of the examination was altogether effaced by Dr. Paul's sensitive professionalism and my own relief.

The problem with my prostate turned out to be minor. The problem with my masculine soul, however, remained significant.

Yes, I gained considerable empathy for women from the experience. I can imagine now how a woman might feel before a male doctor— until relatively recently, her only option for medical care, no matter how sensitive or intimate.

Yet I had always fancied myself to be an open-minded man. Unto today, however, I wonder: was my balking an issue of modesty, just culturally conditioned—or organically apt?

Certainly, in our culture it's not considered manly to be modest. In 1960, showers at my freshmen men's dorm in college consisted simply of six nozzles spaced openly on the wall to accommodate as many men, with a common drain underfoot. Apart from the usual coarse banter in a men's locker room, nobody worried about it—at least, no more than we worried about just getting cleaned up. Our men's PE swimming class was bathing-suit optional, and like several of the other guys, I never bothered to wear one.

I remember, however, a "long distance" lifeguard exercise in pairs, whereby the "victim" assumed a backstroke position, extended his arms straight and placed his hands on the shoulders of the "rescuer," who pushed ahead with a breast stroke between the victim's legs.

Immediately after the demonstration, my partner/rescuer saw what was coming and leapt out of the pool. "But my partner hasn't got a bathing suit on!" he complained to the coach—who in classic coach-ly fashion shot back, "Get back in the pool!" and blew his whistle to begin the exercise. I honestly don't recall feeling any embarrassment; if I did, it would've been for my rescuer's hyper-sensitivity.

MEN'S SHOWER STALLS

Recently during my 50th class reunion, I dropped by that old freshman dorm building, which the Reunion Guide proudly noted had been "remodeled and upgraded." Admiring the now-carpeted hallway and wood-paneled room doors, I noted a sign indicating that women students lived in the building on opposite floors from the men. My old freshman room happened to be on a current men's floor, so I decided to visit the bathroom on my way out. There, I was surprised to see private individual shower stalls, a feature reserved solely for women's dorms back in the day.

Such concessions to male modesty, unto separators between urinals in public rest rooms, betray a gender insecurity which in the old days either didn't exist or wasn't acknowledged. The principality of homophobia would seem to have spoken and its shame accommodated—not to mention its additional construction costs in re-modeling.

I judge not.

Indeed, I'm obliged to note in closing that I've never yet been examined by a woman urologist. The occasion simply has never presented itself. I confess, frankly, that unless I hear clearly from the Father otherwise, I'm not likely to choose such an occasion in the future. It's not about her professional skills, which I would respect, but about my own reluctance.

Again, I wonder: Does this reflect sexism? Unmanly cowardice? Or maybe, appropriate modesty?

I don't know.

I only know that I walked away from my prostate exam years ago with a great lesson. Self-images die hard. In fact, the most cherished of them must die if we are ever to face ourselves as we really are.

And so I no longer consider myself a liberated male—simply one who struggles to submit to women in their competence and to God in His.

In today's sex-saturated culture of exposure, men struggle to see women for their heart and character. We need their help.

7

Miniskirts, Spandex, & Sunday Morning [12]

Judgment, Tolerance, or…?

God gave the law through Moses, but grace and truth came through Jesus Christ. John 1:17

SOME YEARS AGO, SOON AFTER I began pastoring in a laid-back Southern California beach town, I discovered that warm Sunday mornings can stir far more than spiritual fervor.

Anxious to be "culture current," our church fostered a casual style in an effort to model the accepting grace of God. Slacks and sport shirt were fine for the pastor; t-shirts, jeans, and sandals were common among the worship band.

Among the larger, mostly single Sunday congregation, however, an even broader interpretation of "casual" prevailed. Young women sporting their well-toned tan in shorts or miniskirts made an appropriate oxymoron out of the term "barely covered." Skin-tight lycra "bottoms," spaghetti-strap tank tops, and low-cut blouses were common.

In my first months at the church, I was so grateful to be free of my old traditional pastor's coat and tie that I told myself it didn't matter what people wore, as long as they came. God would turn their hearts—and bodies—if we just made His house hospitable enough.

Then one Sunday morning I was seated in the first row and trying to gather my thoughts before getting up to preach. Matter-of-factly, I leaned down to pick up a stray note and glanced down the aisle—and found my gaze lingering. *Lord*, I exclaimed under my breath, drawing back quickly and sitting up straight, *Don't these women realize what they're doing when they dress like that?*

At once, it struck me: Indeed, they know very well what they're doing: seeking men's attention in a manner altogether current in their culture. As the announcements finished and sermon time approached, my dismay gave way to a simmering anger. Quietly, I cried out for grace, got up and plowed my way through the teaching.

Later at home, I sat fuming at my desk. Clearly, we had an unacceptable situation at church and something had to be done about it. But what? And how? And most significant to me, by whom?

For weeks thereafter, a battle raged in my heart and prayers over how the women of our church were dressing—or rather, undressing—for worship. Unspoken in my prayers and shamefully hidden in my heart was the realization that for me to mention the subject at all was implicitly to admit that I was noticing the women's bodies. *note!!*

PASTOR'S CATCH 22

Talk about a catch-22 for the pastor!

Anger was clearly the emotion of choice here. It was flat-out true, I decided, that the women were dressing seductively out of fleshly motives, and needed to be called into account. A glance at a concordance afforded me an arsenal of Scripture aimed at sexual immorality, denouncing such sins of the flesh and exhorting holiness.

Even as I righteously raised my Bible hammer, however, I recalled stories of grace and mercy—of a harlot's washing Jesus' feet, an adulterous woman forgiven.

Was I being harsh, judgmental, and authoritarian?

Indeed, our largely young, single congregation was already ill-at-ease together as men and women. To rebuke the women publicly about their revealing clothes could easily polarize us yet more painfully against each other. Many of the women might well feel offended, become angry, and leave without ever talking it over with me.

Was I wimping out, afraid to challenge sin in our midst?

Nevertheless, the subject needed to be addressed—if only to demonstrate freedom in the fellowship to be real with each other.

I considered a more relational, one-on-one approach. But talking to single women privately about their sexual attraction would be improper for a male pastor, and was clearly out of the question.

How could I bring this word of truth to the women of the church in a way that would not shame them, but rather, demonstrate manly, pastoral respect for them as sisters—even as for the men as their brothers?

At last, a seemingly brilliant idea struck me: I could ask Mary to talk to the women! As a psychologist and Director of the church counseling center, she had ministered healing to many women in the congregation and all respected her. She could just tell them to shape up and dress properly—end of problem!

When I explained to her my dilemma—and my humble desire to bring the women of the church into account—she listened graciously. When I presented my solution, however, she balked.

"Honey," she smiled, ever-so-thinly, "this seems like a real issue for the church, and probably as much for the men as for the women. But I don't sense it's mine to address. It really seems something more for the pastor to deal with. You're still a bit confused over it, so you may need to wrestle it out some more with the Lord."

With a frown and a sigh, I went into my prayer closet—upset that He was not about to let me use my wife as an escape.

At that point, two voices contended in my mind: the classic extremes of "conservative" religious shaming vs. "liberal" universal tolerance. Often over the years I had identified these larger cultural spirits of religion and condemnation vs. universalism and passivity. In fact, I had cast them from myself and experienced a new sense of freedom engendered by Holy Spirit.

NOT ABOUT MORALITY

If I were to enjoy that freedom now—and invite my congregation to do so as well—I knew this issue could not be about either religious theology or universalist ideology, nor even cultural morality. Somehow, it had to be about Jesus, and a Father who loves His sons and daughters so much He sets boundaries to protect us for our created purpose. Painful experience over the years had taught me that, in order to escape the world's consuming extremes and access that place of freedom in my heart, I'd first have to go to the Cross myself and surrender.

And so at last, I fell on my knees and cried out for Jesus to show me this problem through His eyes. Soon, I realized that my great anger and readiness to judge the women as seductive and immoral was at root an effort to cover my shame at the cost of their dignity. In fact, I was dumping my shame on the women instead of taking it to Jesus—who had already borne it on the Cross.

OK, Father, I prayed, *here's the truth: I'm distracted in church by women's bodies. I don't want to be, but I am. I feel ashamed as a husband, a father, and pastor. Forgive me for wanting to unload my shame on the women instead of bringing it to you.*

I hesitated. *Still, Father, I have to say it's not fair! I've worked hard on my own issues, and ministered so much to the other men at church to get healed in our sexuality. They're distracted, too. If you won't take away this brokenness in us men, then what in the world can I say or preach to help you heal us all as men and women together?*

As I sat there alone in my office with the Father, thoughts came to me which I can only characterize as both fearful and wonderful. In a word, I knew what I had to do, and next Sunday was none too soon.

As the announcements drew to a close that morning, I took a deep breath. *Father, help!* I prayed, and glanced around nervously. A bare midriff caught my eye, an angry impulse crossed my heart, and I knew the battle was on. In the name of Jesus, I bound spirits of condemnation, passivity, lust, and denial over myself and the church. I then asked Holy

Spirit to replace those with affirmation, perseverance, purity, truth, and grace.

Moments later, I gathered myself behind the pulpit and looked out over several hundred young men and women, their faces bright from worship and ready for the preacher.

"For some time now…," I began gingerly, "I've been sensing that… that we need to deal with an issue together as men and women. It's not an easy thing to talk about, and even harder to agree on what to do about it."

Uneasily, I looked down at the floor, took another deep breath, then raised my eyes.

"Let me begin by saying to the women of the church that I appreciate how much those of you who are single want a godly man alongside you as a partner. You know very well how much I've ministered among the men to let the Father heal us—to make us the men we long to be and, yes, the men you need.

"I'm proud to say that the brothers here at church have been working hard at getting healed of our sexual brokenness. We're learning to see women not as the world wants us to, as just your bodies, but as God wants us to, as real persons—sisters, in fact. We want to be real men, to come alongside you as trusted brothers, to honor your heart and spirit as well as your beauty.

NO EASY TASK

"I need to tell you that this is no easy task for men today. The culture floods us on all sides with images of half-naked women, from highway billboards to movies, TV, and internet sites. It's a battle. But we're fighting. Really hard.

"This morning, sisters, I want to tell you: We need your help.

"We all appreciate the way we can dress casually for church here. Many of us grew up as kids in churches where that wasn't the case. For us today, dressing casually feels like acceptance and freedom to be who we are and be real together. I, for one, enjoy that!

"We all long for the innocence to accept each other for who we are, not how we look. But we know all too well that we live in a broken world that doesn't always allow that. Until Jesus comes back, we have to learn to be not only innocent as a dove, but also wise as a serpent. Because when we're honest, we know that the world's brokenness is inside us all. The battle to overcome it is tough, and we need each other's support.

"And so, my sisters, I would ask a very big favor of you in behalf of your brothers here at church. Before you come to worship next Sunday morning, would you please look at yourself in the mirror, then look in your heart and ask yourself and the Lord two questions:

"First, 'Does the way I'm dressed this morning encourage my brother to see and know me for my body or for my heart and spirit?'

"And second, 'Does the way I'm dressed this morning help my brother focus during worship on You, Lord, or distract him from You?'

"I respect your relationship with the Father, and trust you as sisters sincerely to seek His word for you. As your pastor, I'm not going to tell you how to dress. But I will invite you to be part of God's healing work among us together as men and women."

I hesitated. Reassured, nevertheless I knew something was still missing. *Anything more you want me to say, Lord?* I prayed quietly. And then, I knew.

"Above all, sisters," I added, "I want you to know that I believe this issue of cleaning out our minds and hearts is our issue as men, and we take responsibility for it ourselves. I hope we've learned from Adam that blaming women for our sin only makes it worse. We're not here to blame you, but to ask for your help."

At last, I took another deep breath and waited.

Murmurs and hesitant glances spread across the room, then a few nods.

"I don't want to belabor the point, so I'll say no more, except that we need to work on this issue together. I hope you'll come to me later and talk over any personal feelings you might have about it."

At that, I proceeded with the service.

Afterwards, several women came up to thank me. "When you first started talking, I wasn't sure whether you were going to jump on us women and tell us we're the problem," one said. "You know—the old craziness like, 'He raped you, but it was your fault for dressing sexy'.

"But you didn't do that. You owned it as a man, and I felt respected. I'll think it over and pray about it before next Sunday."

Buoyed by many similar comments, when the line ended I turned to gather my notes and leave.

Then another woman emerged from the side.

WORKS BOTH WAYS

"I'm glad you had the courage to speak directly to us women about this issue," she declared. Deliberately, she then set her jaw and narrowed her eyes. "But you need to know that it works both ways."

"'Both ways'?" I echoed, puzzled. "What do you mean?"

"I mean," the woman fired back, "that the women aren't the only ones around this church who need to be talked to about exposing themselves!"

Gathering steam, she turned and searched the crowd. Then, like a laser beam, her arm and finger shot out, pointing across the room. "Have you noticed Bill over there in his spandex bike shorts?"

I drew up. "Well, uh, no," I confessed. "Actually, I...I haven't."

"Well, Bill's not the only man here who dresses without thinking how it affects the women during worship. Men come in here with wide shorts, tight sleeveless T-shirts, and all kinds of things that show off their bodies. If you're really sincere about helping everyone get healed, you'll talk to the men of this church the same way you just talked to us women!"

Pausing to digest this new information, I nodded thoughtfully. "Well, OK" I said, gathering myself, "Thanks for telling me about this. I...I'll certainly do that."

And I did. Over the next week, I called Bill, and several other men whom the woman had pointed out, and talked personally to them. Next Sunday at the pulpit, I spoke once again about the issue, this time asking the men to dress with consideration for the women.

Did it work? Did men and women become more considerate in their dress?

It's hard to say.

I only know I sought that elusive balance of both grace and truth which Scripture promises where Jesus is welcomed and given authority. Instead of the Law's fruit in shame, I wanted Holy Spirit's fruit of kindness, faithfulness, and self-control to manifest in our family. I tried to give Father God room to work among us by addressing forthrightly an otherwise covert and potentially divisive issue of sexuality—too often both feared and hidden in churches amid either aggressive conservative judgment or passive liberal tolerance.

I chose to focus instead on relationships in our church family, to demonstrate a trust for one another instead of judgment. I'd never seen that done before, but I would rather give the Spirit more room to work than close others down with the Law.

It's not easy. Father God has given men and women a desire for each other. It's powerful and it's deep. No matter how deliberately and sensitively a pastor speaks to this issue, it will always simmer in any congregation where folks are real.

But just because a task is hard, doesn't imply a license to avoid it.

It's time to get real together as men and women, to stand against the enemy who would use the Father's wonderful gift of sexuality to divide and shame us. I hope my story will stir your church to talk openly about this subject. As you do, ask God to use that occasion to draw all of you close enough to recognize Him as your Father—and thereby, closer to each other as brothers and sisters.

> **I don't want my son to get ambushed by hormones on the way to his destiny.**

8

Cover up Your Daughter—

for My Son's Sake

I have made a solemn promise not to look with lust at a girl. Job 31:1

AS A HIGH SCHOOL FRESHMAN in 1956, I saw a girl's knee as she bent down by her hallway locker and couldn't wait 'til P.E. class to tell the other guys.

Fifty years later, I pick up my son at his high school and see girls standing around matter-of-factly in tight short-shorts, micro-miniskirts, plunging necklines, and low, low-rise jeans—as the girls' track team jogs by in bikini bottoms. Not much left to imagine, or to tell the other guys standing right there.

I'm not shocked, morally offended, or righteously indignant. I'm troubled—because I'm the father of a teenaged young man. I don't want my son to get ambushed by hormones on the way to his future.

I know what you're thinking: This guy's just a dirty old man, hiding it behind a trumped-up concern for his son.

I'll be honest with you. Like my son, I, too, am a man—and therefore, hard-wired for visual stimulation. Like most men, I've battled lustful thoughts. It's hard for us at first glance to see beyond a woman's body to her character. I struggle with that part of myself, and I have a support network of other men where we all work together regularly to overcome it.

Was it so long ago, back in the turbulent sixties, when we all woke up at last and marched for women's dignity? Was it just purple haze when we determined to raise our sons to look at a woman not as an object but as a person, and—to paraphrase Martin Luther King, Jr.—to judge her not by the appearance of her body but by the content of her character?

In fact, I know all too well from my own younger days how consuming and destructive all this girl-gazing can be. That's why I don't want my son to waste himself on it. Instead, I want him to recognize his calling in life, his talents to pursue it, and a woman mutually suited to walk with him in it. I want him to focus his eyes and energies on her, so he can know the joy, both physical and emotional, of genuine love.

Don't tell me as a dad that it's my job alone to do this. Believe me, I'm trying my best. I've talked to him about sex, from menstruation and fertilization to guarding his heart and honoring women (see "Not like Chicken Eggs: Sex Ed 301 for Dad" in *Do Pirates Wear Pajamas?*). To the best of my ability, I've shown love and respect for his mother.

DAD'S NO FOOL

But I'm no fool. When half-naked women leer at him from "family hour" TV and others even less clad are just a mouse-click away, Dad's best efforts are easily trumped by a short skirt across the aisle from him in history class.

Moms and dads, I need your help.

Mothers, if you want your daughter to earn a man's respect, teach her how to act and dress worthy of it. Talk to her about a woman's power not only to draw a man's eye, but to influence his heart.

Fathers, if you want your daughter to discover and fulfill her life's calling, give her a father's blessing, so she doesn't get lost looking for it in the wrong places. "You're such a beautiful young woman, inside and out," you can say. "Wait for a man who can appreciate you, who will honor your heart and uphold your character."

Then tell her how men think: "When you're dressed to show so much of your body, a man can't see beyond that to your character and your heart. He can't know you for who you really are.

"Your girlfriends will all think you're bold. They'll praise you for how cool and hip and daring you look. But that's not what the boys are thinking. They'll judge you as cheap, quick, and easy."

Sure, beauty in His daughters is one of Father God's marvelous gifts to this world. By all means, Dad and Mom, affirm your daughter's beauty. Tell her she's pretty. But—contrary to what our sex-addicted culture dictates—tell her it's not the only gift a woman bears.

Above all, therefore, please: affirm your daughter's heart. Name the good things you see in her character. Highlight her talents and abilities, and encourage her to develop them. Tell her she deserves the best, and if she acts like it, she'll get it. Reassure her that as she remains true to herself, in good time the right man will be drawn to her for who she is and not just for how she looks.

Warn her, however, that if she displays her body as the most important part of herself, men will heed that message. They'll compromise her character and trash her heart.

In fact, men are not primarily drawn by excessive exposure. Years ago as a cub newspaper reporter, I was assigned to interview young women for a feature story on "How to Attract a Man." One wise and attractive bank teller quoted early film star Mae West, "What they can imagine is better than anything you can show them."

SEXUAL IMPROPRIETY

Even thousands of years ago, as in the opening chapter Scripture, the ancient Job struggled with lustful eyes. Some things don't change— except that some men, like Job, are more real than others.

Once, as my son got in the car after school, I asked him point-blank, "How do you handle all the girls showing so much like they do?"

Sighing, he shook his head helplessly. "You just have to get used to it."

Determined to preclude the shame of religion, a secular culture has no option but to de-sanctify sexuality—and thereby prohibit the wonder, the awe, the pleasure, the joy, and the excitement of its power.

I rage against a world that does this to my son—and grieve a Church that has allowed this by abdicating its witness to the spirituality of desire.

Since apparently no one else these days is speaking in behalf of men about sexual exposure, let an old man say it here: Femininity blossoms amid security. When her nest is neat and safe and paid for, when her relationship is trustworthy and caring, the woman feels free and responsive. *New line.*

Masculinity, on the other hand, thrives amid the challenge of insecurity. When he doesn't know whether his team will win or lose, whether the business deal might close or not, whether she'll say Yes or No for a date, the man feels challenged to overcome his fears and excel.

At my age, I may not know what's hot, but I know what's not.

To a young man, the young woman who publicly unveils herself insults him. "With me," her body language scoffs, "the insecurity—all the mystery, fear, and challenge that stirs true masculinity—is gone. There's nothing to pursue in me or overcome in yourself, no need to know my heart or share my life's calling. You don't have to do the work of winning me, because you're not man enough to do it.

"With me, the adventure is over as soon as it begins."

My son deserves better.

And so does your daughter.

> When the enemy calls for your mind and eyes, you want to be able to say, "You're too late. I don't have anything left of myself to give you, because I've given it all to the Father."

2

No Yellow Elephants

Controlling Uncontrollable Desire

Sin must no longer rule in your mortal bodies, so that you obey the desires of your natural self. Nor must you surrender any part of yourselves to sin to be used for wicked purposes. Instead, give yourselves to God, as those who have been brought from death to life, and surrender your whole being to him to be used for righteous purposes. Sin must not be your master; for you do not live under law but under God's grace. Romans 6:12-14

AS ADULTS, WE MAY LAUGH at my back-of-the-school-bus sex lesson in the Introduction. But it's a nervous laugh, since the inherent mystery of sexual attraction does not resolve itself after puberty. In fact, it only becomes more evident and challenging as we "mature" and seek to control our lives.

I learned this after teaching about sexuality at the tender beginnings of my men's conference ministry, when a man in the audience raised his hand tentatively.

"So…how do we get control of, you know, our eyes and thoughts and all that?" he asked.

Seizing my Bible righteously, I lifted it high. "You've got to know the Word of God!" I charged.

Amid a confused silence, the man raised his hand again. "Yes, but…," he managed, uncertain, "Jimmy Swaggart knew the Bible…."

Steeped in religion, I knew the right answer—but not the real answer.

Not long before that conference, TV evangelist Swaggart had been caught with a prostitute, issued a tear-filled apology on his show—and awhile later was caught yet again with another prostitute.

Indeed, before my conference inquisitor that day, I was humbled. Struggling to defend myself, I realized quickly it was no use. "You're right, brother," I could only allow. "I need to pray this issue through some more!"

As I did that later, I remembered that Swaggart's cousin was 1950s rock 'n roller Jerry Lee Lewis, whose career imploded when he married his thirteen-year-old cousin. Both Swaggart and Lewis—even Lewis' underage wife—shared the same grandfather and sabotaged themselves with sexual impropriety. Very likely, a spirit in their bloodline was driving their sexual appetites. Like so many Christian men today, Swaggart knew the Bible but didn't know the Father who wrote it, because his own father-wound blinded him (see "To Know the Father" in *Healing the Masculine Soul*).

Swaggart's fall therefore sounded at first like a contradiction: How could someone so gifted in ministry fall so hard to sexual temptation?

WEAK SPOT

As I later became exposed to spiritual warfare, however, I realized that it made all too much sense. In fact, the very anointing and power in Swaggart's ministry drew the enemy—who knew his generational weak spot in sexuality and therefore attacked him precisely at that point.

The names of equally anointed ministries whose founders have fallen are legion. When Colorado mega-church pastor Ted Haggard, President of the National Association of Evangelicals (2003-06) was caught in a homosexual affair, the predictable righteous outrage and unrighteous rationalizations filled the media—and missed the point entirely.

As I wrote in a Letter to the Editor of *Charisma* magazine,

> I'm concerned that I haven't heard one Christian leader yet say that this tragedy has caused him to gather his own platoon of brothers and get real with them to deal with his own deepest struggles.
>
> It's as if Christian leaders are riding around on their bicycles without helmets and one falls and cracks his skull open. They all rush to come alongside him, get him to the hospital, comfort his family, and cover his ministry responsibilities—but none of them go get a helmet.
>
> If any Christian man fancies that "this could never happen to me," may he live happily ever after. Haggard's particular sin may not be your own, but every one of us men is a small step away from destruction without the grace of Jesus and the supporting presence of honest and caring brothers.
>
> The sad truth is that the only men who are accountable are the ones who want to be.
>
> Now, at last, Haggard wants to be.
>
> Do you?

Sadly, my estimation of Haggard's humility and desire for healing was presumptuous and naive. Soon after the obligatory apologies and a brief three weeks of "counseling," he was back pastoring at a new church.

Once again, shame trumps truth, short-circuits healing, and helps the enemy recruit another servant of God.

Today when men ask me how they can control their sexual desires, I answer directly, "You can't. In fact, you don't control any spiritual power. Only Jesus does that, precisely insofar as you surrender to Him." Self-control, in fact, is a "fruit of the Spirit" (Galat. 5:22). It's not the natural result of your effort, but the supernatural result of God's effort (see "Beyond Fig Leaves and Cooties: Loving a Woman" in *Sons of the Father*).

In the Kingdom of God, we're not held accountable for our sin nature—any more than a cat for chasing a bird—but precisely for not defying its shame, crying out to Father God in its grip, and receiving the grace He's given us in Jesus to overcome it.

JUST SAY 'NO'?

"You think you can control yourself whenever sexual temptation comes?" I ask at my men's conferences. "You say you can turn it off any time you want—like, 'Just say No!' and forget about it? That sounds great.

"And I command you now, Do *not* think of a yellow elephant! This is a commandment. I don't want any man here thinking of a yellow elephant! NO YELLOW ELEPHANTS—do you hear me?"

As the men stir with confused smiles, I nod convincingly. "The more I command you *not* to think of a yellow elephant, the more you do. Most of you right now have a herd of yellow elephants stampeding in your brain!"

Merely commanding yourself not to do something has no real power to stop you from doing it. Often, in fact, that stirs you to do it. "It was the Law that made me know what sin is," as Paul declared.

> If the Law had not said, "Do not desire what belongs to someone else," I would not have known such a desire. But by means of that commandment sin found its chance to stir up all kinds of selfish desires in me. Apart from law, sin is a dead thing. (Rom. 7:7,8)

"Suppose you see some woman getting out of a car in a miniskirt," I explain to the men. "You can command yourself for the rest of the day,

'Don't think of that woman's legs! I put that woman's amazing legs out of my mind!' It sounds religiously correct, and you can beat yourself with it all day. But when your head hits the pillow that night, guess who comes to visit?

"You didn't ask her to come, you didn't want her to come. But it's the devil's game: the more you think and talk about her legs, the more of a stage you give the enemy to perform."

Significantly, Scripture here uses the term "desire" and not "need." In our more surrendered moments, that distinction seems trivial. Sin, however, always seeks justification to avoid both its shame and the conviction which would drive the sinner to the Father. Among a generation weaned on the world's self-centered values, therefore, the distinction becomes crucial.

NO SEXUAL NEEDS

I once counseled a young man in my church not to have sexual intercourse with his girlfriend. "But Pastor," he protested, "I have my sexual needs!"

"My brother," I responded, straining for grace, "I can't soft-pedal this. I can only tell you flat-out: There's no such thing as a 'sexual need'."

The young man drew back almost in shock, as if I uttered blasphemy—which, of course, I did, at least in the context of today's popular self-worship.

"Give me an example of something you need in order to live," I offered.

Gathering himself, he indulged me. "Well, of course, there's air, food, water, protection..."

"Exactly," I declared. "If you don't have those things, you die. But no one's ever died from lack of sex!"

Yes, my reader, I know it can feel like that at times. I understand. But trust me, you'll survive. There's more going on in life than your desires—in fact, far better than what you want. But to receive and embrace it, you need to prioritize and pursue what God wants for you.

If we allow for "sexual needs," the debate is pre-empted and the issue of whether to restrain your sexual energies is moot. There's no room for another viewpoint, not even God's. "You need it" means you've got to have it and you're right to get it.

Rather, we have sexual desires. This term allows for choices—which opens the door to mature responsibility and mutually respecting relationship with God and each other.

Even as a wolf smells blood, the enemy will focus most convincingly where you're most vulnerable. You can't overcome his attack in your own natural strength. But you can choose to recognize unhealthy desires and cry out for Jesus to save you amid them.

"It's faith that welcomes God to go to work and set things right for us," as Paul exhorted the church at Rome.

> This is the core of our preaching. Say the welcoming word to God—"Jesus is my Master"—embracing, body and soul, God's work of doing in us what he did in raising Jesus from the dead. That's it. You're not doing anything; you're simply calling out to God, trusting him to do it for you. That's salvation. (Rom. 10:8-11TMB)

"It's like hydraulic brakes," as the late Argentine evangelist Juan Carlos Ortiz put it. "You apply the intention and God provides the power."

SEXUAL ADDICTION

I once ministered to a young 23-year-old man Alan (not his real name) who struggled with sexual addiction. Pornography, anonymous one-night stands, and prostitutes ruled his life. As we prayed together, he cried out to the Father to overcome the consuming cravings which seized his mind and body. Over several months of meeting weekly, he confessed sin and received forgiveness, re-visited old childhood family wounds with Jesus, cast out associated demons, and committed to a discipline of his eyes and mind.

Eventually, Alan began to recognize the enemy's deceptive temptations and experience Holy Spirit's power to ignore or resist them. We were both amazed at his progress.

Then one day he told me that several apartments near the swimming pool in his complex had been rented to an Italian women's volleyball team for the summer.

Oh, no, Father! I thought. *This could sabotage all the healing we've worked so hard for!* With a measured sigh, I tried to mask my fear—but only betrayed my lack of faith. "That must be a…a challenge," I offered.

To my surprise, Alan smiled knowingly. "What a joke!" he laughed. "At first, I couldn't believe all those hot women around the pool in bikinis. I mean, it was off the charts, after all the sex stuff I've been through. And then I realized, this is so over-the-top—it's obviously a set-up."

Shaking his head in self-dismay, Alan chuckled again. "Ha! I can't believe the enemy's that stupid to be so blatant about it and try to steal all the healing I've gotten and everything I've learned. Like I wouldn't see what's going on! I just laugh about it and go on with my life."

"Yeah, that's…that's sure ridiculous, alright," I managed—with a quick grin to cover my shame. *Forgive me, Father, for not trusting your work!*

As so often happens, the devil overplayed his hand. Thankfully—as too often doesn't happen—Alan trusted his Father, turned away from the enemy's distraction, and pressed ahead with His calling.

What's more, I learned a valuable lesson through my shortcomings: A healthy sense of humor can trump self-restraint and save a lot of energy!

Laughing at the devil, of course, requires a secure relationship with the Father, knowing implicitly that He stands alongside you with power to deliver you from the enemy's schemes. It's a good sign, and a good option.

But certainly, we don't always have that measure of faith. When you don't, as a starting point in overcoming lust it's helpful to believe not just that you have a natural impulse to miss God's mark, but that He's present to help you hit it.

FOCUS UPSTREAM

Yes, I believe we're accountable to God for a sinful act. But in order to overcome the desire to sin, you need to focus upstream on its root.

The primary issue is not whether we'll sin, because it's in the fallen nature of this world to call us away from God and in our own fallen nature to follow. Rather, it's whether we'll have a close enough relationship with Father God to discern thoughts and actions that miss His mark and to seek humbly His saving power when such sinful urges call.

"You can't stop the birds from flying overhead," as Martin Luther once said, "but you can keep them from making a nest in your hair." In this fallen world, that is, you can't stop sinful sexual impulses from entering your mind, but you can choose not to welcome and host them.

The foundation of victory lies in knowing God's heart is for you, that when He tells you not to do something, it's therefore for your own good. He's not a spiritual slave master out to deny you pleasure, but an ever-present Father who wants to protect you from pain (see "From Law to Love" in *Fight like a Man*).

As the temptations become strong, you can quit giving the yellow elephants a stage and instead cry out to God for saving power: "Father! I give up—not to the temptations, but to you. Please, take these thoughts. Please come and overcome this distraction from you and from the person I want to be."

As Paul exhorted the Corinthian Christians,

> It is true that we live in the world, but we do not fight from worldly motives. The weapons we use in our fight are not the world's weapons, but God's mighty weapons, which we use to destroy strongholds. We destroy false arguments; we pull down every proud obstacle that is raised against the knowledge of God; we take every though captive and make it obey Christ. (2 Corinth. 10:3-5)

"Easier said than done!" you might say—and I can only agree. It's war, and war is always tough. The battle for God-ordained sexuality, however, is not ultimately between you and the devil, but between you and the Father—who has authority over powers below as well as those above. The more power you give God to change your actions, the less power you have to give the enemy to entrench them.

TOO LATE, SATAN

In fact, whatever portion of yourself you don't give to the Father of Truth is fair game for the father of Lies. When the enemy comes calling for your mind and eyes, you want to be able to say, "You're too late, Satan! I don't have anything left of myself to give you, because I've given it all to Jesus."

Yes, you need to be ready to face and cast out enemy spirits when the Father calls you to do that. Amid the fear and confusion of attack, however, it's easy to focus on what the enemy is doing instead of what God is doing. When temptations come, check in first with your Commander-in-Chief—who alone can direct your victory. The first move of faith is not counterattack, but rather, surrender to Jesus—who came precisely "to destroy the devil's work" (1Jn 3:8NIV; see "First, We Surrender" in *Fight like a Man*).

Sometimes, Holy Spirit may direct you to fight back in His authority, to name the enemy spirit that's frustrating God's purposes, identify its source, and cast it out. Other times, He may show you an enemy spirit in yourself that needs to be confronted and evicted, or an unhealed wound which allows it entry. He may lead you to a reassuring promise in Scripture and tell you to wait on Him to act more manifestly. Sometimes, it's just your old Adam sin-nature calling.

You can get exhausted from fighting when you don't see any victory, and wonder if God's doing anything at all. That's when all your work building relationship with Him pays off. The future is always uncertain. But what your Father has done in the past stands. Because He's already seen you through so much pain and fear before, you can have faith He's with you even now.

Thus,

> When he lived on earth, anticipating death, Jesus cried out in pain and wept in sorrow as he offered up priestly prayers to God. Because he honored God, God answered him. Though he was God's son, he learned trusting-obedience by what he suffered, just as we do. (Hebrews 5:7,8TMB)

With that freedom to be real with your Father, you can just cry out for Jesus and hold onto Him—trusting that He's working out His purposes in and through you as you stay open to Him. "Remember that I have commanded you to be determined and confident," as God spoke to Joshua on the threshold of Jericho. "Do not be afraid or discouraged, for I the Lord your God, am with you wherever you go" (Joshua 1:9).

It's helpful—though frustrating, granted—to remember that the Father's purpose is often greater than removing your pain. Warriors, however, understand and accept that the greater victory often requires greater suffering and sacrifice.

Be humble enough, therefore, to know you need others alongside you in the battle. Even as soldiers go to war not singly, but rather, together in a platoon, the struggle to stay pure with your thoughts and eyes requires meeting regularly with others for support and prayer (see "The Wolf Loves the Lone Sheep" in *Sons of the Father*). Fasting is a particularly helpful spiritual discipline for discovering how much your natural appetite and desires are controlling your life, and for humbly releasing control to God (see "The Weapon of Fasting" in *No Small Snakes*).

Resisting temptation is a challenge worthy of God's calling. But there's another dimension to the problem of controlling sexual desire in our own strength.

SUPPRESS OR STOKE

Amid today's sexual frenzy, it seems that if we're not trying to suppress desire, we're trying to stoke it.

"OK, I may not be able to turn it off," as one brother countered at a conference. "But I can turn it on any time I want!"

For such accomplished performers, I ask, "How many of you men here became fathers 'by intention'—you know, when your wife and you want to get pregnant and try hard to make it happen?

"If you did, you likely know that she can go to the local drug store and buy an 'ovulation timing kit' for just a few dollars. By the miracle of modern chemistry, she can tell just when that egg is ready for you.

"Now, if you fancy yourself to be 110% eager and responsive, I challenge you to imagine your wife standing in front of you with an ovulation timing kit in one hand—and a stopwatch in the other. 'It's now or never!' she demands. 'Five, four, three, two...'."

Pressure to perform does not enhance the excitement. When it's all about commandments and clockwork, in fact, a man can often feel anxiety—and nothing else.

"Uh, honey, could we maybe...slow things down a bit?"

"Look who wants to slow things down!" the wife exclaims. "Mr. Jack Rabbit himself wants to take time!"

"Well, maybe we could just talk about it, you know...?"

"Look who wants to talk all of a sudden! Mr. Clam Up And Hide In His Cave wants to communicate!"

Like I said, a little humor can take the edge off.

In any case, every honest man knows it doesn't always happen. That's because we're not talking formula here, but spiritual phenomenon. In fact, when a man fails to get aroused, the last thing he needs is "The Five Biblical Commandments of Godly Sexual Performance" posted above the marriage bed.

Nothing smokes out the pretensions of religion like sexual "performance." The rules and punishments of religion may identify the sin, but can't stop the urge to sin nor save you from its effects.

Here's some advice for a man when performance fears arise: Take time to tell your wife what you like about her. (Appreciation funds can be donated the next morning through my website.)

FREEDOM TO RESPOND

In fact, when a man feels safe with the woman, his fear of failure often fades. When physical intimacy is an occasion not to perform but to enjoy, there's freedom to respond. Even if you don't get aroused, deeper intimacy can come from mutual understanding and acceptance. "Doesn't look like this is our night," you can say. "So let's just hold each other awhile and look forward to next time."

Certainly, a healthy lifestyle of exercise, nutrition, and avoiding drugs, smoking, and excessive alcohol is as important to sexual response as to any other physical activity. Sometimes, one or both of you can just be tired or stressed. Maybe you need to talk through a difficult issue together but have shut down out of fear the other won't listen.

Because sexual desire is fundamentally spiritual, its dysfunction is more often rooted in emotional and spiritual issues than in physical health. See your doctor, but be sure to pray and ask the Father what's going on.

Shame lurks here. Feeling safe with your spouse can have more to do with your own fears than with the other's responses. If you've been wounded by someone of the opposite sex in your past, you can seek inner healing prayer to restore openness.

Whatever the reason, if you worry about performing sexually, you can go to Father God and get real: "Father, I give my sexual desire to you. I can't control it. I can't make it happen or make it turn off. I'm tired of worrying either that it'll get out of hand or won't show up. I put it in your hands and trust you to quicken me according to your will."

Then exhale deeply, and release it all to God.

After that, you can ask Him, "Is there any emotional or spiritual issue that needs healing here?"

In some cases, both men and women may find themselves chronically unable to respond. Here, deeper emotional and spiritual healing is often necessary. In a man, such impotence is often rooted in being wounded by his mother as a boy and/or shame from Dad that undermined his self-confidence as a man. Similarly, frigidity in a woman can come from being wounded by her father as a girl and/or shame from her mother which undermined her self-confidence as a woman. An experienced Christian counselor can help to heal your childhood wounds, refresh your heart, and free you to respond to your spouse.

When both husband and wife go humbly and openly together to Jesus for healing, shame flees and the Father's grace flows. The enemy has no hooks with which to manipulate them against one another, and the Father has room at last to work His healing in each of their lives. His victory comes when brokenness that the enemy wanted to use as a weapon to divide the two thereby becomes instead an avenue to deeper understanding and intimacy.

SPLITTING OFF

A word of caution: The fear of not performing can tempt you to fantasize some other, ostensibly more arousing experience besides the present moment. Visions can range from pornography to an earlier relationship or even a previous occasion between the two of you.

Splitting off from the moment, however, is the problem, not the solution. Often, you learned to disengage when childhood pain or fear overwhelmed you. Those who were sexually molested as children are especially vulnerable to this impulse to escape reality. Certainly, drugs and alcohol can suppress such pain, but in doing so, alienate you from your partner and suppress sexual desire as well.

Jesus has a better plan, namely, to heal the wound and use that process to draw you closer to Him and to each other. In fact, Father God can heal those memories when you ask Jesus to stand with you in them.

I once ministered to a young woman who for no apparent reason feared getting close to her fiancé. When we prayed and asked Jesus to reveal the roots of that fear, Holy Spirit surfaced a scene from eighth grade, when her best friend's father exposed himself to her. Though she was able to run away, that experience traumatized her (see Healing Emotional Wounds: Seeing the Past as Jesus Sees It," in *Broken by Religion, Healed by God*).

When we prayed further, she asked Jesus to enter that scene and in her mind's eye He led her at last to stand boldly before the man and tell him how his actions had harmed her. Eventually, Jesus showed her the man's own wounds that had led him to try and abuse her, and she was able to forgive him. This cleared the way for her heart and body to respond appropriately to her fiancé.

Sexual intimacy brings mutual joy when both partners are present in the moment, surrendered to God, and trusting Him to lead. Overcoming sexual dysfunction—whether in turning it on or turning it off—is often a process of renouncing its shame and surrendering your desire and response to the Father.

Whether you're single or married, you can begin that process with simple, humble trust in Him.

A GOOD HUG

When Mary and I began dating, for example, we were strongly attracted to each other. Both of us had made relationship mistakes in the past. Because we knew more deeply than ever that God had called us together, we wanted to honor Him and each other with appropriate boundaries. We wanted to give Him as much room as possible to work in our life together.

On our first date, as we went up the walkway to her apartment door, I began praying under my breath, *Father, what do you say—can I kiss her?*

"A hug would be good," I sensed.

I hugged her and said Good Night.

On our second date, I prayed on the walkway and sensed the same word. Again I hugged her and said Good Night.

On our next date, after Disneyland and talking together about our future plans, I prayed yet again—but this time sensed nothing. Uncertain, as we reached her door, I asked one more time, *Father, can I kiss her?* In that moment, no word came, simply a glowing brightness. I believe the Father was pleased with us both and was beckoning in delight.

I kissed her.

And the man said, "It is good."

Mary and I didn't want to repeat harmful relationship patterns from our past. The attraction between us was powerful, but we were determined to face our issues together and not allow sex to short-circuit the healing God was doing in our lives. By His grace, we were able to maintain faithful boundaries during our courtship.

It wasn't easy. Before long, the time came when somebody had to call Time Out. I had made the mistake of not doing that in past relationships and wanted to demonstrate my confidence in how much more significant this one was. I wanted us to be healed and ready for all the Father had planned for us in our marriage.

Even as a surgeon would keep you on the operating table, I wanted to stay within the Father's boundaries so our hearts could be as cleaned out and open as possible to receive that. And so I told Mary that I would take responsibility then and in the future to raise the Stop sign, because I didn't want to pre-empt the Father's power to grow our relationship.

"Thank you," Mary said. "That means a lot to me. In other relationships, I've always had to play the policeman. Knowing I can trust you like that allows me to let down my guard and feel like a woman."

Thankfully, with that encouragement from her and much grace from the Father, I was able to keep my word.

The fountainhead of sexual faithfulness lies not in your partner, but in the Father, whose Spirit is present, active, and powerful to keep you within His boundaries. It's not about biting the bullet in order to keep the Law, but surrendering to the Father in order to experience His power and grace. When you realize you're not capable in your natural ability to rule your desires, that is, you're ready to put them back in God's hands— even as Jesus did on the cross and was resurrected in the fullness of His Father's purposes.

Thus, Paul declared in the opening scripture that we don't have to beat ourselves up for having sexual desires, nor to disqualify ourselves from God's blessing by missing His mark. "Sin must not be your master; for you do not live under law but under God's grace" (Rom. 6:14).

As we'll now see, honoring God's boundaries in a relationship is not about morality or even righteousness, but about spiritual protection for His larger purposes.

> **Sexual union causes a spiritual bond between the partners which natural human power cannot break—for better or worse.**

10

What God Has

Joined Together

Spiritual Consequences
of Sexual Union

There's more to sex than mere skin on skin. Sex is as much spiritual mystery as physical fact. As written in Scripture, "The two become one." Since we want to become spiritually one with the Master, we must not pursue the kind of sex that avoids commitment and intimacy, leaving us more lonely than ever—the kind of sex that can never become one. 1 Corinth. 6:16,17TMB

IN ORDER TO CONFRONT Barry's overwhelming attraction to his girlfriend (Chapter 3), I knew that simply exhorting him to abstain from sex, no matter how biblically endorsed, would not trump the compelling electricity between them. Young singles awash with hormones demand— and deserve—something at least as real and compelling to check their desires. They need to know why a loving God who creates the wonder of sexual attraction does not want them to express it fully before marriage.

Too often, Christians shrink from this challenge. Rather than seek God for His deeper perspective and purpose, we hide from open, honest discussion behind religious dogma, moral pronouncements, and judgment.

Respect for the power of sexuality and those who struggle with it—namely, all of us—demands a visceral debate. In abdicating, we only confirm the popular accusation of hypocrisy, namely, that we Christians ourselves are overwhelmed by our sexual energy and have no power—or credible reason—to limit it.

And so I leapt in. "Are you having sex with Sally?" I asked Barry matter-of-factly, striving for a balance of truth and grace.

"Mm-hmm," he replied, nodding with delight, albeit restrained before his pastor.

"Have you had sex with other women in the past, before Sally?"

"Well…, yes," Barry allowed hesitantly, not sure where this was headed.

"How many other women?"

Pausing thoughtfully, he knit his brow.

"Listen, Barry," I said, interrupting his calculations. "Let's cut to the chase. Now that you're with Sally, do you ever think about any of those past women?"

No need to knit his brow on this one.

"Yes," he replied. "To tell the truth, it seems like those old memories are always there." Gathering steam, he noted that "There was Jane and Barbara and…"

"OK," I interrupted again. "Have you ever wondered why you still think of those past partners, even when you're with 'the woman for you' now?"

"Well, of course, Sally has her times, you know, when she's not in the mood. I don't want to go with other women, so I just remember things in my mind."

PAST MEMORIES

"So past memories of other women come up when you're with Sally?"

Barry paused thoughtfully. "Well…, yes," he noted.

"Do you ever wish you didn't think of those other women?"

Barry said nothing, his silence speaking for him.

"When you open the door to old memories," I noted simply, "it's sometimes hard to close it." Pausing to let Barry know I wasn't trying to force my agenda, I then eased ahead.

"Listen, Barry, I'm happy that you're excited about Sally. I can see that your relationship with her is really special and you want to keep it that way. If you're serious about this relationship, I can help you to stay focused on her and love her even when she's not in the mood—and to avoid getting distracted by women in your past."

More intrigued now than cautious, Barry nodded. "Yeah, that would be good."

"The fact is," I noted, "all women have their 'times'. If you really want to love a woman and receive her love, you're going to have to get real and push through this issue someday, with some woman. If Sally's really the one for you, this is a good time to begin."

Like Barry, few of us today were ever taught that sexuality is "as much spiritual mystery as physical fact," as the Apostle Paul explained millennia ago in the above scripture. What's more, that mystery includes a bond deeper and more lasting than any physical touch, verbal commitment, or legal contract.

It's eternal.

In fact, even as our faith commitment is to "become one with (Jesus)," sexual bonding causes a spiritual bond between the partners. That's why Barry kept thinking of his past relationships even when he was with Sally.

Lest we in our secular stupor forget, time in the spirit realm is not subject to our natural limitations. "There is no difference in the Lord's sight between one day and a thousand years," as Peter declared (2Pet. 3:8).

Spiritual bonds last forever. Human power can neither amplify nor nullify them, nor can any human agency break them. That's why a loving Father God doesn't want His children to have sex outside of marriage: because *acts that have eternal consequences are not designed for temporary commitments.*

Of course, even if you're now divorced, sexual union with your ex established a spiritual bond between you. Your state court system, that is, declares in a legal certificate that you and your spouse are married. If you divorce, the state issues another document to "finalize" the split.

But it's not finalized in your heart or spirit. Being no longer bound by legal documents doesn't mean you never think of the other person again—nor indeed, of your sexual experiences together. Long after you've broken up, in fact, the deep bond formed by intercourse remains to sponsor a free-flow of spiritual forces between you and your ex, even as with other past sexual partners. (see "How Demons Enter—and Leave" in *No Small Snakes*)

It's like the Russian and American space modules when they meet and connect with a crawl tunnel. Cosmonauts can then move freely over to the American ship and astronauts can access the Russian craft. It's free-flow, for better or worse. The mission is both enhanced by everyone's expertise and endangered by their shortcomings.

SPIRITUALLY TRANSMITTED DISEASE

Similarly, in sexual intercourse, whatever spirituality resides in the man flows into the woman; what's in the woman flows into the man. Couples need to be careful, therefore, about the spiritual power that comes into their hearts, since it will reside there and affect you for a long, long time. What's more, it will affect others with whom you have sexual relations. Doctors know STDs as Sexually Transmitted Diseases, but your heart knows STDs as Spiritually Transmitted Diseases, which can "infect" you from sexual partners who carry them.

Thus, for example, a spirit of abuse often enters a woman who has been raped. Thereafter, it broadcasts from within her. Many abused women are therefore abused again later, because their natural discernment and defenses have been compromised. One such woman I ministered to feared salesmen because she felt unable to resist their sales pitch (see "Kick Me Spirits" in *No Small Snakes*).

If you have sex with her, that spirit of abuse can enter you and stir impulses to treat her with disrespect or otherwise abuse her—and others. Certainly, you're still responsible for how you treat her and can't blame the devil if you mistreat her. But if you want to stop the dysfunction at the source, you need to identify and cast out the spirits which fuel it.

In the same fashion, a man abandoned by his father can carry a spirit of abandonment. If he has sex with a woman, that spirit can flow into her, and she will struggle against an impulse to abandon him (see Ps. 27:10).

Singleness, therefore, is a season ordained to prepare a couple to walk out their destiny together. Ideally, they abstain from sexual intercourse, as a fast, in order to confess and be cleansed of sin, healed of emotional wounds, and delivered of evil spirits. This protects them from defiling one another, confusing evil spirits with Holy Spirit, and sabotaging God's plan for them.

When thus prepared, the couple seal the covenant together with God in a public marriage ceremony and later consummate it sexually. Thereupon, the fullness of God's Holy Spirit in the man can now flow freely into the woman, and the fullness of Holy Spirit in the woman can flow into the man. A powerfully equipped and mutually enhanced team thereby emerges to fulfill their ordained roles in establishing God's Kingdom.

Sadly, in our spiritually blind, sex-addicted culture, this divine goal is rarely acknowledged, much less achieved. The enemy of God, meanwhile, is literally hell-bent to sabotage such Godly union and its mission. All too often, couples don't begin this journey into readiness until their sins, wounds, and demons have sufficiently threatened if not destroyed the relationship.

CORINTH TODAY

The ancient church at Corinth, to whom Paul wrote the opening text to this chapter, was situated much like today's church in a larger culture that worshipped sex. The Corinthians were just more honest about it, and therefore more graphic than we are.

Ancient peoples, that is, understood that when enough people attribute saving power to a particular spiritual entity, that entity takes up residence among them. Eventually, it grows into what Paul called a demonic "principality" which rules over the territory where it's worshipped as a "god" or "goddess" (Ephes. 6:10).

Today, for example, the principality of lust rules over Los Angeles as a Hollywood suburb. In my city of Santa Barbara, the more refined spirit of sensuality infuses the beaches, art galleries, and upscale living. Further north in San Francisco, where same sex attraction is celebrated, a spirit of confusion rules. Where shame is so deep that the dominant culture must fabricate an "inferior" people compared to whom they themselves can appear OK, the principality of racism presides (see "The Mirror of Prejudice" in *Broken by Religion, Healed by God* and "Victory over Racism" in *Fight like a Man*.)

In Corinth, the ruling principality was the goddess/demon of lust, named Aphrodite—from which we derive the word *aphrodisiac*, for sex-enhancing substances like Viagra. At the entrance to the city harbor, a large statue of the naked goddess welcomed visitors; "In Corinth, let the sailor beware," was a common saying among seamen in the ancient world.

TEMPLE PROSTITUTES

As one study Bible introduces Paul's letters to that church,

> The city boasted an outdoor theater that accommodated 20,000 people...and the great temple of Aphrodite with its 1,000 prostitutes. The immoral condition of Corinth is vividly seen in the fact that the Greek term *Korinthiazomai*

(lit. to act the Corinthian) came to mean "to practice fornication."[13]

This culture informed Paul's congregation—and therefore, his ministry to the Corinthian church.

The Jewish/Christian place of worship was called a temple. In his sermons, therefore, Paul had to be careful to distinguish God's temple from that of Aphrodite. This dilemma perseveres. I once read a film critic who declared that, "In Los Angeles, the churches look like movie theaters and the theaters look like churches."

Unadulterated by modern secularism and spiritual denial, the Corinthians acknowledged not only the spirit realm, but that its powers manifest graphically in sexuality. Accordingly, in their worship of Aphrodite they sought to conjure sexual experiences, and "ordained" both male and female "temple prostitutes" to do that with "worshippers."

A vulgar display, to be sure. Nevertheless, Corinthian temple worship reflected a spirituality often more vital and genuine than in our modern Western world—where few people, even in churches, believe the spirit world exists.

With such over-arching lust co-opting Godly worship—like today's bikini models on highway billboards and couples having sex on movie screens—Paul preached forthrightly. "You know that your bodies are parts of the body of Christ," he wrote in another translation of the opening text (TMB). "Shall I take a part of Christ's body and make it part of the body of a prostitute? Impossible!

"Or perhaps you don't know," Paul continues—speaking even more powerfully to our spiritually ignorant audience today—"that the man who joins his body to a prostitute becomes physically one with her? The scripture says quite plainly, 'The two will become one body'." Paul then concludes with both the promise and warning that worship creates a spiritual union with its object: "But he who joins himself to the Lord becomes spiritually one with him."

APHRODITE LIVES

Aphrodite yet lives. Today, for example, we could substitute the word "pornography" for "prostitute," as many use a pornographic image to masturbate and thereby, bond spiritually with it. The ancient Corinthians simply lacked such virtual accoutrements.

Years ago when Mary and I were working with a medical fertility specialist to become pregnant, I was required to "provide a sperm sample." I was told it needed to be "fresh," and thereby, "produced onsite" at the clinic. At my appointment, the nurse handed me a vial and directed me to a small room, noting that "there are some things to help you there."

Uncertain, I opened the door and entered the room cautiously. There, to my dismay, pornographic magazines lay worn and strewn about the couch. "Welcome to Corinth" might as well have been proclaimed on the door.

What a pathetically ignorant culture! In the absence of true spirituality, amid the abdication of Christians who alone can know and proclaim it, we behold Aphrodite. At a time when the man needs most to bond with his wife in the glorious mystery of fatherhood under the aegis of Father God, instead he unites his body and spirit with a full-color foldout prostitute.

With a prayer for spiritual protection, I went back to the nursing station and promised instead to fulfill my requirement at home.

Even as Paul preached authentic spirituality to a culture lost in demonic deception, our world today needs desperately to know the truth about spiritual bonding via sexual contact. What's more, we need to know that the Father revealed in Jesus doesn't just judge and abandon us in our sin, but indeed, intervenes to save us from its effects.

If human power or agencies cannot break these spiritual "one-flesh" unions, how then can we become freed from them and stop being affected by past sexual relationships?

Pioneering Christian pastor/author John Sandford cites Paul's words above when he notes that "any complete sexual act, whether fornication, adultery, homosexuality, or some other aberration, unites a person's spirit with the other." Thereafter, "our spirit still remembers that union and seeks to fulfill, nourish, and cherish the other." Thus, "if there have been many immoral unions with many partners,

> our spirit becomes like an overloaded transformer,
> trying to send its current in too many directions.
> Having been delivered by confession, absolution
> and prayer for separation, counselees have often
> cried out, "I have never felt so free. I didn't realize

how scattered I felt. I feel together again." Of
course! Their spirits were no longer having to
search heaven and earth to find and fulfill dozens
of forgotten partners.[14]

I might add to this blessing that their spirits are freed to focus on
and unite with the suitable companion of God's choosing in marriage,
and accomplish thereby the purposes for which He called them together.

BREAKING ONE FLESH UNIONS

When I minister this teaching, whether to an individual like Barry
or to a conference audience, many thank me for a "new sense of freedom."
Here's how I lead a prayer to break such "one-flesh unions." Keep in
mind that this is not a formula, but a guide to help focus your thoughts:

1. "I confess my sexual sin of (lust, fornication, adultery, pedophilia,
pornography, homosexuality, etc.) and ask you to forgive me for not
trusting you, Father God, when you said it would separate me from you
and your good purposes." Fornication, of course, does not apply to a
divorced partner, since you were covered by the marriage covenant—
unless you had intercourse together before marrying.

Often, people will ask me, "But we didn't really go all the way—does
that count?" Remember, we're not talking legal standards, but spiritual
connections. Jesus defined adultery not simply in physical terms but as
even looking at another person with lust (Matt. 5:28). A spiritual union
can occur without "complete" intercourse, and even without physical
contact if the desire to bond is not checked.

For those who are not sure whether a bond was formed, ask Jesus.
Often, if you have to ask, it likely was. If you're still not sure, it can't hurt
to include that contact in your prayer list.

2. "In the name of Jesus, I renounce and disown the spiritual bond
between me and (my partners) in those sins. I want no more spiritual
access between us."

This declaration aligns your will with the Father's will. It may seem
simple, but the flesh has held onto those bonds for a reason—as, for
example, when Barry wanted to avoid the discomfort with his current
girlfriend during her "times." You need to disavow any and all false

"benefits" which the enemy would offer to seduce you away from the Father's blessing in your present or future relationship.

3. "In the name of Jesus, I take the sword of the Spirit and I cut those spiritual bonds between me and (name of partner/s)." If you don't know the names of some partners—as for example, in the pornographic images—you can simply say, "between me and that person/the person/ those persons in the magazine or film."

4. "I release those persons to you, Jesus, and put them in your hands to deal with as you choose."

This prayer is no license to contact former partners, but to separate you from them. Certainly, if you have children with your ex, you want to maintain cordial relationship together for the children's sake. But you do not want spiritual access between you any more.

5. "The blood of Jesus cleanse me from all effects of that union/ those unions."

On the cross, Jesus took the burden of our sin on Himself, so we would have free access to Father God and thereby, the ability to start afresh in a future relationship.

6. When ministering to one person alone as opposed to a larger gathering, ask Holy Spirit to reveal any demons which entered him/her from those sexual partners and cast them out. For example, you can pray, "In the name of Jesus, I set the cross between me and (partner), and I bind you spirit of fornication and cast you out of me into the hands of Jesus."

The one-flesh union opens a spiritual channel between you and your partner, through which spirits of all kinds—not only of a sexual nature— may have entered you. In fact, these and other associated demons from one-flesh unions will pass down to your children if you don't go to Jesus for deliverance. Finally, ask Father God to fill the space left vacant by the evicted demon with a counterpoint from His Holy Spirit—such as purity, faithfulness, and dignity as a son/daughter.

8. Even as you have turned over your past partners to the Father, now surrender your own body to Him. Lay down your sexual desire at the cross, as a Manufacturer's recall, and give it back to the One who created it. Trust Him to restore it in His time as best for you, and to lead you into the future He has planned:

"I now put myself in your hands, Father. Cleanse my desires to be used for your purposes. Reveal those purposes according to your will and give me what I need to fulfill them." As Paul concluded,

> So then, my friends, because of God's great mercy to us I appeal to you: Offer yourselves as a living sacrifice to God, dedicated to his service and pleasing to him. This is the true worship that you should offer. Do not conform yourselves to the standards of this world, but let God transform you inwardly by a complete change of your mind. Then you will be able to know the will of God—what is good and is pleasing to him and is perfect. (Rom. 12:1,2)

Healthy sexual expression for a woman is not about guilt and shame, sin and obedience, nor even promise rings and rituals. It's all about the Father's love for His daughter.

<u>11</u>

Was It Good for You (too), Dear?

Sexual Bonding and a Woman's Heart

God looked over everything He had made; it was so good, so very good! Genesis 1:31TMB

Mary Andrews-Dalbey, PhD

IN 1953, ALFRED KINSEY PUBLISHED his groundbreaking *Sexual Behavior in the Human Female*,[15] which marked the beginning of today's "sexual revolution." Published before the advent of oral contraception, the report was "immediately controversial among the general public," according to Wikipedia. "The findings caused shock and outrage, both because they challenged conventional beliefs about sexuality and because they discussed subjects that had previously been taboo."[16]

What was so shocking about Kinsey's report? From his interviews with approximately 6000 women, Kinsey learned that "women and men are more alike in the biology of their sexuality than was previously thought, and that both men's and women's sexuality seemed shaped, not merely repressed, by social and cultural forces."[17]

Christianity has been a social and cultural force for almost two thousand years. Could it be that the Church has not only repressed, but also shaped our ideas about sexuality? The adjective "puritan," for example—taken from that Christian communion in the early 1600's— has today come to mean one who "asserts stern morality" and "regards pleasure as sinful."[18] The strong influence of such earlier church movements leads us to ask, Have sexual attitudes even among modern Christians—especially women—been shaped by both the Church and the larger secular culture?

The sexual revolution birthed the famous question, "Was it good for you, too?" So that's what I want to ask and explore. No, not as in an episode from *Sex and the City*, but as in sexuality and your self-image. For both women and men, that is, sexuality often both determines and reflects how we feel about ourselves.

After all, God made us female and male in His image, and commanded us to "be fruitful and multiply" even as Adam and Eve were "naked and not ashamed" in Paradise. What's more, He said that what He created was "very good." Sounds to me that God made sex not only for reproduction, but also to enjoy.

MARIANISMO

As a little girl, I was raised Catholic—more precisely, in the Mexican Catholic tradition. For those of you not familiar with my culture, one word aptly describes it for women, *marianismo*—first used by political scientist Evelyn Stevens in her 1973 essay "Marianismo: The Other Face of Machismo."[19]

In order to maintain the dominant male, or *macho* hierarchy, the culture demands the opposite role for women as revered in Mary, the Virgin Mother of God—that is, one of submission and chastity. As complements, *marianismo* and *machismo* cannot exist without each other. The former dictates the day-to-day lives of Mexican women: cleaning, cooking, and serving men. Stevens believes that this *marianismo* will not disappear anytime soon because many women still cling to this female chauvinism.

Building on Stevens' work, researchers Jorge Villegas, Jennifer Lemanski and Carlos Valdez conducted a study on the portrayal of women in Mexican television commercials.[20] Their study revealed a significant difference between the portrayal of dependent women and independent women, namely, that "Dependent women tended to display characteristics perceived as positive in *marianismo* whereas independent women were more sexualized." Here's the classic Madonna-whore dichotomy prevalent in the Mexican culture: the former is esteemed as barefoot and pregnant at home, while the latter serves the baby's father with sexual flings.

As a first-generation college-educated woman, I had to work through my cultural issues in order to overcome a seven-year "all-but-dissertation" author's block and complete my doctoral program. Yet as I reflect on my background, I realize that the *marianismo* mindset in the Mexican Catholic culture also manifests today in some Evangelical circles which foster a male-dominant, *machismo* worldview.

A blog by Samantha Field reflects this counter-balancing in noting how "purity culture" and "raunch culture" are opposite sides of the same coin, because both objectify women.[21] Similarly, in *Female Chauvinist Pigs: Women and the Rise of Raunch Culture*,[22] Feminist Ariel Levy examines our over-sexualized American society—which not only objectifies women, but in fact encourages women to objectify themselves as a form of female empowerment.

Witness, for example, the media transformation of young actress Miley Cyrus from teeny-bopper ingenue Hanna Montana to today's coarse and grinding pop star. "Hanna Montana Is Dead" read a recent concert poster among cheering twenty-something fans, apparently seeking more power than the wholesome character of their girlhood allowed.

Purity/modesty culture, on the other hand, describes the prevailing church teachings to women—as, for example, to "kiss dating good-bye," wear a purity ring, appropriately cover your female body, and pledge your virginity to your father.

OBJECTIFY WOMEN

At first glance, the church modesty culture exhorts women to flee the over-sexualized influence of today's media in order to save themselves for their future husbands. The church culture thereby attempts to protect women, while the media-charged culture exploits women. In reality, however, both cultures objectify women.

A sentence has a subject, a verb, and an object. The subject acts upon the object; the subject is active while the object is passive. In social psychology, objectification means treating a person as a thing. Sexual objectification means treating a person as an instrument of sexual pleasure. To objectify women simply means to see women as a sex object to gratify the subject.

Thus, the "madonna-whore" dichotomy. The church modesty culture uses guilt and shame to exhort women to cover themselves modestly and uphold standards of virtue. Yet the media raunch culture also uses guilt and shame to pressure women in the other direction, namely, to uncover themselves, "courageously" break free from tradition, flaunt their sexual power, and aspire to unrealistic *Playboy* standards of appearance and behavior.

The church culture seemingly reins in the natural lusts of godly men, while the media culture feeds them. Both cultures, however, portray women as objects.

In a nutshell,

> Modesty culture fosters a fear of sex by controlling women in order to rein in men's lust. It's repressive.

> Raunch culture fosters a fearlessness of sex in order to please men, and in that sense, to excite men's lust and thereby manipulate them. It feels powerful and liberating.

Both views focus on responding to men's sexuality, not on honoring the integrity of women's sexuality.

DAD'S MODEL

This objectification of women can be rooted in a girl's relationship with the first and foremost man in her life, namely, Daddy. Fathers, that is, can reinforce it by what they *model* to their daughters in their own reaction to women. What young girls see their fathers *do* matters more than what they hear their father's *say*.

Many clients have told me that they observed what kind of women their fathers were attracted to, and that's what they would strive to become. Unfortunately, these women were not talking about their mothers. Rather, they noticed as young girls how their father's eye wandered while they drove down the street, and what he was sneaking to see online or in a magazine.

A few women described to me how their fathers even bragged to other male friends about their young daughter's sexual attractiveness. Dad's objectification of women often inflicted their daughters with deep sexual brokenness later in life via promiscuity and an inability to bond with a husband. This caricature of women as sex objects transfers from generation to generation.

Fathers must teach women that their beauty is more that skin deep—not only by their words, but more importantly, by checking their own lust.

Father God declares our beauty and power as women by His Spoken Word. He has formed "wonderfully" our "inner parts" and breathed His Holy Spirit into us (Psalm 139:14). When Father God sees a woman, He doesn't see a body to satisfy a man's physical desire. Rather, He sees a daughter, even an heiress to His Kingdom, created to satisfy His desire for her fulfillment.

Recently, I told Gordon that I wanted him to see me as God sees me. Gordon said that he wanted that himself, and prayed, "Father, please show me Mary as you see her."

Waiting for a moment, he then told me, "I see you standing tall wearing a regal purple robe and a crown on your head. In your right hand, you're holding a shaft like a sceptre."

HOW GOD SEES WOMEN

Indeed, Father God imparts stature, beauty, and authority to His daughters. That's our true identity in Christ and our role in His Kingdom. In order to overcome the objectification of women, we need to embrace how God sees us. It's not about purity culture vs. raunch culture; it's about God's Kingdom and living within the grace and truth of His rule.

Years ago, I read two books that profoundly changed my understanding of the Bible: *There Were TWO TREES in the Garden*[23] by Rick Joyner and *The Subversion of Christianity* by Jacques Ellul[24]. Each emphasizes that the forbidden tree in the Garden of Eden, known as The Tree of the Knowledge of Good and Evil, encompasses the knowledge of Good as well as the knowledge of Evil. It's not Knowledge *per se* that separated us from God, nor was it the knowledge of Evil alone, but rather, the deciding ourselves "what is good" and "what is evil."

Religion epitomizes this primal heresy, because its insistence on correctness beckons self-righteousness and division—which distracts from our genuine need for God's Holy Spirit to give us discernment.

Life, meanwhile, is in the other tree—the Tree of Life—which is Jesus, who pre-empts the vain striving of religion and draws us freely to the Father.

Both polarities of "free" unrestrained sex and restrained, forbidden sex therefore separate us from the life that God intended when He created man and woman. To idolize sex, as today's pop culture, distracts from God's purposes, but to say sex is fundamentally sinful and evil, as traditional religion, blasphemes against God's creation. Ultimately both mindsets rob women of the joy in their sexuality that God intended.

Many Christian prohibitions on sex were established centuries ago by the early Church. These restraints served the political, economic, and religious interests of the male-dominated establishment.

Long before the Kinsey report, men in the early Church knew and feared the power of women to stir sexual desire and therefore, shame and guilt. Even after a woman was no longer considered her husband's property, the patriarchal Church sought to control women through religion. Believing that celibacy was the prime Christian vocation, leaders projected their own frustration onto women, whom they castigated as evil temptresses.

The early church writings of St. Augustine in the fourth century illustrate his own sexual conflict after leaving a worldly lifestyle to be a celibate priest.[25] Unfortunately, his struggles introduced significant shame into Christian attitudes towards sexuality.

BETTER SEX

At Creation, however, God said that sex was good, in fact, "very good." I believe that married women can therefore have better sex than singles and that married Christian women are the most capable of sexual fulfillment. Sadly, this doesn't seem to be the norm today.

I do not mean marriage makes sex *better* simply in the physical sense, but *better* because (a) it's how God designed sex; (b) it's integrated with the woman's whole being, and therefore, (c) it leads to intimacy in all aspects of life itself: physical, emotional, and spiritual. For a woman, that's what enables sexual fulfillment.

I remember my single years as a pastoral counselor at a predominately single church. All too often, the unmarried women complained about having to be celibate while the married women grumbled about feeling obligated to have more sex.

What's wrong with this picture?

Having survived that single season myself and experienced 25 years of married life, I believe we've missed the mark.

Yes, missed the mark—that is, we've sinned.

Sexual desire was created by God and is good. God's purposes for sex are unequivocally good. Rooted in the knowledge of good and evil, however, religion distorts God's view by seeing sexuality in itself as sinful and shaming our natural desire.

By God's design, human beings have an innate desire for intimacy. Certainly, that includes the physical desire for sexual relationship. But it also means a desire to know and be known, to love and be loved. In fact, the best relationship is one that has all three elements. For a woman, sexual intercourse is only one ingredient that contributes to true intimacy.

More fulfilling sex requires not only desire, but communication, love, and commitment. That's why marital sex is better. For women especially, sex protected by the marriage covenant enables us to feel desired, chosen, accepted, and cherished. Security in her marriage enables a woman to surrender freely, to receive and to be sexually fulfilled. That freedom makes her more apt to experience orgasm.

VULNERABLE AND SAFE

Sexual intimacy, at its best, makes the partners vulnerable to one another. Yet, vulnerability typically requires trust amid security and stability together. In order to become vulnerable, a woman needs to feel safe—not just physically, but emotionally as well. We don't want to be judged, devalued or rejected if we open our hearts. Without this protection, sexual activity can leave us lonely, isolated, disoriented, cynical, and afraid to trust, because our sexuality is the most vulnerable part of a woman's identity.

Scripture uses the phrase, "Adam knew Eve" when referring to his having intercourse with her (Gen. 4:1RSV). Indeed, sex exposes the most vulnerable part of who we are. When a women gives herself to a man, she's allowing herself to be fully known. When a woman waits until marriage, she demonstrates self-care, because it protects her from being used, that is, from being known and then cast off and forgotten.

If a man cannot commit to a woman in marriage, he's not giving her the emotional security that she needs to surrender fully to him. He's saying that he wants to keep his options open in case someone more desirable shows up later. This wounds a woman's heart.

I therefore urge my women readers, Protect your heart. If a man tells you he's not ready to commit, BELIEVE HIM. Don't conjure false hopes and try to make him commit, or expect him to be more responsible.

Sexual encounters without commitment damage a woman's spirit. Research shows that women who engage in serial relationships often suffer from depression.[26] To bond and be known deeply and then disconnected over and again, inevitably takes a toll on a woman's self-esteem.

That sounds antiquated, I know, but it's just how women are wired. We need to be reminded of this so that we can protect and care for ourselves. That's why our Father God tells us to wait—not because He wants to deny us pleasure, but because He wants to save us from pain. In order to wait faithfully for marriage, a woman must feel worthy of a man's persevering after her. That worthiness requires that she be willing and able to receive God's love.

Healthy sexual expression for a woman is not about guilt and shame, sin and obedience, nor promise rings and rituals. It's all about the Father's love for His daughter. Can we receive His love? Can we love ourselves as God loves us? "We love because Father God first loved us," as John put it. "And we ourselves know and believe the love that God has for us" (1 John 4:16,19).

ECONOMICS OF SEX

From an economic viewpoint, we might argue that sex is about acquiring valued "resources" as much as it is about seeking pleasure. The average woman attempts to acquire things she values in return for sex—such as love, attention, status, self-esteem, affection, commitment, and emotional bonding. Indeed, women's sexual activity often has an unspoken exchange value.

Men's sexual activity more likely does not. That's because women are most often the sexual gatekeepers within their relationships and decide when sex begins. In general, women can have sex when they wish to; men can only hope for it.

This "economy," however, might be contrary to how most women feel. They don't think they control the sexual aspect of their relationships. Many young women feel that they have to trade sex for relational stability or for any relationship at all. Often, the man and woman negotiate sex within their own social context according to what couples around them are doing and not according to what's best for the woman herself.

Contrary to their expectations, therefore, women tend to lose power when they initiate sex quickly in a relationship. In doing so, they basically hand men the keys to the future of the relationship.

Of course, sex without security sounds fun! Women might be taught—by friends or media—that they can have sex "like a man" without the need for all those strings attached. Popular TV shows perpetuate this fantasy—like *Sex and the City, Grey's Anatomy, Coupling,* and *Forty Something.* It looks exciting; everyone must be doing it!

In reality, however, it's just plain hard to accomplish and sustain that lifestyle. Those women are acting! Real women simply aren't wired that way. For real women, emotional bonding and the "strings attached" are what make sex good.

It's hard for a woman to deny her heart and force herself not to care. Promiscuity destroys a woman's sense of integrity and well-being.

In fact, sex without strings is illusory. All sex has "strings attached." The strings of intercourse are real and impacting; they bond us together physically and spiritually, whether we like it or not.

Sexual contact binds you to your partner's spirit, creating a "one-flesh" union (Mark 10:7,8). That spiritual union bonds the man's and the woman's spirits as one and continues even long after the relationship has ended. "There's more to sex than mere skin on skin," as Paul put it:

> Sex is as much spiritual mystery as physical fact. As written in Scripture, "The two become one." Since we want to become spiritually one with the Master, we must not pursue the kind of sex that avoids commitment and intimacy, leaving us lonelier than ever—the kind of sex that can never "become one." There is a sense in which sexual sins are different from all others. In sexual sin we violate the sacredness of our own bodies, these bodies that were made for God-given and God-modeled love, for "becoming one" with another. Or didn't you realize that your body is a sacred place, the place of the Holy Spirit? Don't you see that you can't live however you please, squandering what God paid such a high price for? The physical part of you is not some piece of property belonging to the spiritual part of you. God owns the whole works. So let people see God in and through your body. (1Corinthians 6:16-20TMB).

HORMONAL BOND

In fact, the hormone oxytocin is released in the brain during sexual intercourse. This same hormone is released during breastfeeding and bonds a mother to her infant.

This hormone helps a woman bond similarly with a man. When she and a man touch each other in a loving way, oxytocin is released in her brain. It makes her want more of that loving touch, and she begins to feel a bond with her partner. Because it's a chemical reaction, it becomes an involuntary process that can't distinguish between a one-night stand and a lifelong soul mate.

Oxytocin can cause a woman to bond with a man even during a short-term sexual relationship. So when that relationship abruptly ends, the induced spiritual connection shatters. The emotional fallout can be devastating.

On the other hand, there's good news in oxytocin. Its hormonal bonding effect is ideal for marriage in fostering trust, commitment, and security even through difficult times.

Father God loves His daughter and wants to protect her heart. His design for sex within the boundaries of His marriage covenant demonstrates His love and commitment to her. A woman reflects that blessed spirit of daughtership when she owns those boundaries for herself and waits for the man who respects her enough to maintain them himself.

Those whose innocence was stolen from them as children seek to steal it back by uniting sexually with a child, the bearer of innocence to this guilty world.

12

Pedophilia

The Lust for Innocence

So Jesus called a child, had him stand in front of them, and said, "I assure you that unless you change and become like children, you will never enter the Kingdom of heaven. Matt. 18:2,3

What's more, when you receive the childlike on my account, it's the same as receiving me.

But if you give them a hard time, bullying or taking advantage of their simple trust, you'll soon wish you hadn't. You'd be better off dropped in the middle of the lake with a millstone tied around your neck. Matt 18:5,6TMB

PAINFULLY, ALAN (NOT HIS REAL NAME) lowered his eyes and shifted in his chair as he told of being sexually molested as a boy. In my ministry, I hear such stories all too often, but this time words burst forth like a bombshell in the night, illuminating the root of this diabolic, crippling experience.

In his mid-forties, Alan had been plagued by passivity and simmering anger throughout his life. As we prayed together for God's healing presence and power, I invited him to close his eyes and recall that awful childhood scene, call out for Jesus to be present with him in it, then speak out as to his perpetrator the feelings he had so long buried in shame.

"Yes, I can sure remember that place and what happened there," he declared, closing his eyes. "Jesus, please—come and be with me here!"

After a moment, Alan began to tremble. "Jesus is...standing beside me and I'm...I'm looking up at Mr. X," he noted, leaning forward. "Thank you, Jesus. Yes, I...I need you here. I'm really scared!" And then, clenching his teeth, Alan drew up in determination. "I hate you Mr. X for what you did to me!" he murmured, seething.

"Tell him exactly what he did that makes you so angry," I urged, wanting to uproot the deepest aspect of this wound.

"You...you," Alan began—then hesitated, struggling to put his feelings into words. "YOU STOLE MY INNOCENCE!" he shouted at last, raising his fist.

Awe-struck at this thunderous truth, we both sat transfixed as a commanding silence fell upon us. Then slowly, as from a dam bursting, Alan lowered his fist and fell sobbing into his hands.

When eventually Alan gathered himself, he asked Jesus to show him Mr. X from God's perspective, and saw Mr. X's own deep childhood wounds. This enabled Alan to forgive Mr. X. With that foundation, I led Alan in a prayer to break the one-flesh union from the molestation.

We then asked Holy Spirit to reveal the spirits which had leveraged that trauma in Alan's life—including pedophilia, abuse, homosexuality, man-hating, worthlessness, shame, despair, distrust, rage, and self-hatred—and cast them out, replacing them with Holy Spirit's agency of love, affirmation, purity, brotherly love, dignity, hope, compassion, and trust (see "How Demons Enter—and Leave" in *No Small Snakes*). Alan had much healing yet to do, but this experience laid the foundation and gave him courage to pursue the Father for it.

LOSS OF INNOCENCE

The Genesis story of creation portrays the loss of innocence as the root malady of our human condition. That's why Jesus came: to cover our sin nature with His blood, enable us thereby to approach God freely and openly as Father, and receive through His Spirit what we need to fulfill His created destiny for us. In fact, Jesus highlights the child as the organic beacon of innocence and in that sense, His reflection in this dark and guilty world.

"Who is the greatest in the Kingdom of heaven?" His disciples asked Jesus.

> So Jesus called a child, had him stand in front of them, and said, "I assure you that, unless you change and become like children, you will never enter the Kingdom of heaven. The greatest in the Kingdom of heaven is the one who humbles himself and becomes like this child. And whoever welcomes in my name one such child as this, welcomes me." (Matt. 18:1-5)

At the beginning of life, God separated Adam's body into male and female in order to invent relationship. But the primal memory of their Original unity remained within their hearts, lingering in a compelling sense that a missing part of each lay outside, in the other. "That is why," the Bible concludes, "a man leaves his father and mother and is united to his wife, and the two become one flesh" (Genesis 2:24, NEB). Made of the same body, that is, both man and woman long to go back to that same one-body-ness, as in The Beginning.

Hence, sexual attraction—ever flourishing among us as it promises literally to restore us to Paradise. Candlelight dinners, romantic ballads, and Valentine's cards are but a pale reflection of the innate human longing to walk once again in wholeness and innocence before our Creator God.

From our very Genesis, when "the man and his wife were both naked, and they felt no shame," sexuality and innocence have been framed together as mutually enhancing and interdependent (Genesis 2:25 NIV). When our hearts are clean and our motives pure before God—when our commitment to one another in marriage is as eternal and devoted as God's commitment to us—sexual union bears no shame, but indeed, divine grace. In fact, its unmatched pleasure and joy remind us of Whose we are as it restores us to the one-ness we were when God first created us in Adam.

In their physical union under God's intention, the two thereby become open and free as children before a loving, protecting parent. We eat from the Tree of Life.

A man and woman therefore seek each other in order to reconnect with, and in that sense, regain the wholeness which was lost to them at creation. After the Genesis split, sexual desire reflects a longing to take back into yourself something you lost, and focuses on the other person who literally embodies it.

The dimension of the man's self lost to him in the split, we call femininity; the dimension of the woman's self lost to her in the split, we call masculinity. Thus, the man seeks sexual union with the woman in order to regain the femininity lost to him since Creation; the woman seeks sexual union with the man to regain the masculinity lost to her since Creation. In sexual union, they return to life as it was holy and wholly in the Beginning—reflecting in their oneness the very image of God: "So God created man in his own image…male and female He created them" (Gen. 1:27NIV).

Thus, the man and woman become "suitable companions" to fulfill God's purpose for them, as they each contribute to the union complementary giftings which only the other has.

AVENUE FOR RESTORATION

God has provided the avenue for restoration to that wholeness, namely, Jesus. "There is therefore no condemnation for those who are in Christ Jesus," as Paul declared (Rom. 8:1). On the cross, He bore our shame, restored our innocence before God, and saved us for God's purposes. No longer do we need to bear it ourselves unto death and hide in fear of either divine or human rejection. We can again be "naked but not ashamed" before God and each other, open and trusting like children (Gen. 2:25).

In fact, when we humbly cry out our brokenness and need before Jesus, "God's Spirit joins himself to our spirits to declare that we are God's children" (Romans 8:16). This joining of spirits and its fruit both in bearing children and their child-like freedom complements the joining of bodies as man and woman.

Similarly, in the Eucharist, or sacrament of communion, we take into ourselves the body and blood of Christ, who was without sin—literally in a *co-union* which harkens unto the "one flesh" covenant of marriage. Thus, we seek organically to unite with Jesus, to take Him into our bodies, in order to regain from him the innocence that we lost in turning from God at Creation. "This is my blood, which seals God's Covenant," as Jesus declared at the Last Supper, "my blood poured out for many for the forgiveness of sin" (Matt. 26:28).

The traditional Church definition of a sacrament is "the outward and physical sign of an inward and spiritual grace." When at creation the man and woman trusted the Snake instead of God's protective boundaries, they suffered, rather, a *dis*-grace. Significantly, the outward form of their inward *disgrace* was the covering of their genitals. The "embarrassment" which men and women feel at being naked before one another is therefore not a learned social behavior readily overcome by public nudity. Rather, it's a primal, existential reality which reminds us of our inability to overcome the powers of the world—both within us and without—apart from divine grace.

Ever since Adam and Eve ate from the Tree of the Knowledge of Good and Evil, humanity has suffered a natural inclination to turn away from our dependence upon God. We gave up the child-like trust and vulnerability that we enjoyed in the Garden, and were thrust out into a knowing world of good and evil. From our very Genesis, therefore, human life has been animated by a crippling fear of shame and a longing for restored innocence.

INVESTED IN DENIAL

As our sin nature filled the world, meanwhile, humanity threatened not only to become comfortable in guilt, but in fact, so invested in denial as to forget what innocence looks like. In order to draw us back to Himself and our true Genesis prior to the Fall, God needed to provide a clear and enduring model of innocence. What could God offer humanity to hold that memory of innocence alive—even sufficiently engaging as to make us want it back and seek after God to restore it?

Enter the child: helpless, powerless, without self-consciousness or guile; open and trusting, receptive and hopeful, free and vital (see "Can

Daddy Come out and Play?: The Ministry of the Child" in *Do Pirates Wear Pajamas?*).

Like Jesus, the child comes to restore innocence. That's why Jesus has such an affinity for children, even as to identify them with Himself. "To such as these," he declared, "belong the Kingdom of God" (Matt. 19:14).

Clearly, in an adult world hell-bent to cover its shame, the child's innocence becomes an extremely valuable commodity.

Insofar as we don't trust Jesus to restore our innocence, we fabricate it ourselves. The most visible form of that effort throughout world history has been religion—that is, behavior standards and moral obligations which, when presumably attained, erase your sin, confer God's approval, and thereby, restore innocence. But such efforts to seize initiative from God, dismiss Jesus' sacrifice, and cover shame by ourselves only sabotage the authentic, child-like humility and trust which defines the Tree of Life.

As the story of Adam and Eve's fall portrays, when we allow the voice of shame to override the honest cry for mercy, we not only lose our divinely ordained innocence, but become compulsive later in seeking to regain it, as via religion. Indeed, if you don't turn humbly to Jesus to receive His restoration, you can become infected with a desire to seize innocence—as, for example, in racism, whereby you cast your shame onto others and fancy you're OK insofar as they're not OK.

STEALING INNOCENCE

Those who do not trust God's work in Jesus will therefore be compelled to fabricate innocence—if not by religion, racism, or other human means, then by stealing it. Thus pedophilia is motivated by a desire for restored innocence, and the perpetrator seeks sexual union with a child in order to regain it from the child.

In a judgmental, shame-based family or culture, a child's innocence is destroyed by shame. Even as a child raised in poverty might imagine no way to gain money besides stealing from the rich, a child who suffers shame and punishment may seek to gain innocence as an adult by stealing from those who richly bear it—namely, children.

Certainly, this mis-focus requires a disconnect from Jesus, because He is not only the living source of innocence, but he came precisely to give it freely. It's called grace—something children reared in shame rarely experience.

It's as if you're thirsty and see someone with a glass of water. Instead of going to the fountain yourself for a drink, you steal the person's water.

Often, in fact, most pedophiles have been molested themselves as children. As Alan declared, their innocence has been stolen from them. In order to get it back, Father God calls you to receive it back from Jesus, the source. The father of Lies, however, calls you to steal it from another child (see "To Know the Father" in *Healing the Masculine Soul*).

Thus, a news story in my local paper reported a 40-year-old man arrested for molesting a 5-year-old girl. The police interview said he "stated 'It was like payback' for being molested himself as a child."[28]

Similarly, a Catholic priest who molested numerous boys at a parochial school in our town was described as "The product of an alcoholic, volatile father who served in the military and a scared mother. As a boy, the priest had attended the same school and was himself molested there by a priest."[29]

"Thou shalt not steal" is one of the Ten Commandments not because it's immoral to steal, but because it's unfaithful, reflecting a false image of God. Thieves steal because they don't believe they can get what they need by asking (the Father) for it. Similarly, pedophiles seize upon children because they don't trust Jesus to restore their innocence via humbly confessing to Him their need for it.

Religion often hosts this deception in fabricating a virtual innocence by urging sacrifices, correct behavior, and right belief to placate the deity. Such motions of religion become the most accessible hiding place for those consumed by shame.

The God revealed in Jesus, however, does not want our human sacrifices. "Go and learn what this means," as Jesus charged His religious detractors, "'I desire mercy, not sacrifice'. For I have not come to call the righteous, but sinners" (Matt. 9:13NIV).

In Jesus, God has provided for our deepest human need, namely, for restored innocence and thereby, trusting relationship with our true Father. It's a gift for the asking, called grace (see Rom. 3:21-24).

What if, indeed, Jesus has borne our shame on the cross? Then we have no need to hide it. You can come out of your sin-closet, fall at his feet, and cry out for his mercy. There, you can receive His restored innocence, go freely to Father God, and by His grace get what you need to recognize and fulfill your destiny.

JEALOUS OF CHILDREN

Because so many adults today were wounded emotionally as children and their needs were not met, our pain-avoidance culture dares not recognize those needs. A child's innocence, that is, stirs the painful memory of when we were children and our own open and trusting hearts were wounded. We therefore cannot respect children's innocence and in fact, envy them for it. A jealous world assaults it mercilessly—from kindergartner bikinis to violent cartoons and video games.

The father of Lies, aka prince of Darkness, seeks most diligently to hide God's work or distort His image. He therefore hates children, because their innocence is the most authentic reflection of God's Kingdom in this world. The more we withdraw from the genuine innocence offered by Jesus, the more we will resent it in children, crush their hearts with shame, and sabotage their witness to the Kingdom of God among us.

Innocence is the fruit of the Tree of Life, embodied by Jesus. It's therefore most readily destroyed by shame, the fruit of the Tree of the Knowledge of Good and Evil, embodied by religion. Thus, the religious establishment engineered Jesus' death, as so often even today. (see "Blackmailed by Shame, Healed by Truth and Grace" in *Broken by Religion, Healed by God*). Shame and a longing for restored innocence is most deeply internalized by those oppressed by unattainable demands— as in religion.

Ultimately, therefore, healing pedophiles is neither about punishing sin with condemnation nor destigmatizing it with tolerance. It's about deep childhood wounding and a child-like trust in Jesus to restore innocence by overcoming the effects of sin.

> **A man getting married or about to become a father needs the blessing and grace of other men who have walked the path ahead of him.**

13

Tasteful Gifts Only[27]

Bachelor Party Redeemed

Taste and see that the Lord is good. Psalm 34:8NIV

THE INVITATION CAME on a simple white card, but was unlike any I'd ever seen:

CHRISTIAN BACHELOR PARTY
(Tasteful Gifts Only, Please)

Before becoming a Christian, I'd been to enough bachelor parties to identify raunchy, taste-less gifts. But in all my years as a Believer, including pastoring for over ten years, I'd never seen Christian men celebrate a brother's upcoming marriage. As a new member of this church, I was intrigued to find out what the men had planned.

I arrived a little late, only to find men wandering aimlessly around what turned out to be some very tasteless Christian punch. Chatting around the refreshment table, I noticed the upcoming groom as Guest of Honor off to the side, seated on the edge of the couch by himself, uncertain and more than a bit pale.

I paused, punch-in-hand, as an often-repeated image leapt to mind from my days as a pastor: A young man in stiff-collared tuxedo stands sweating in my office before his wedding, his closest allies gathered about him for this overwhelming commitment at hand. Trying his best to cover his fear and avoid its shame in male company, the groom turns his back to the rest of us and gazes out the window. His suited groomsmen chat nervously, wanting to help their beleaguered comrade, but themselves at a loss amid the life-changing mystery of marriage that beckons all men.

As the fateful bells chime and organ calls, inevitably the Best Man takes a deep breath and steps toward his friend. Resolutely, he stumbles ahead with a strained smile, slaps the groom on the back awkwardly and asks for all to hear, "Are you scared?"

Shame-out-loud is no comfort to a man at that moment. But as a seasoned pastor—and married man myself—I had learned to be ready.

"I hope you *are* scared," I would interject. "If you're not, there's something wrong with you. Getting married is a big step, and none of us men has all the answers here. But it's something we all want, so let's all take a minute to ask the Father to bless our brother here for the great adventure ahead of him."

With that, I gather the friends around the groom to pray. After thanking God for bringing him together with his bride and for all family and friends gathered to support him, I ask the Father's blessing on this day and on their marriage.

GET US GOING

A sip of ginger ale laced with Hawaiian punch sputtered me back to the present. Looking again at our uneasy Guest of Honor, I began to pray. *Father, come on—surely you want to use this occasion to bless the groom and not just have us standing around like this. We've never seen any men do this before and don't know how to make it happen. Do something to get us going!*

Almost immediately, a wild idea popped into my mind. I hesitated, then decided to walk over to the host and draw him aside.

"Thanks for getting us all together to honor Joe," I offered. "What made you think of doing this?"

"Well, hey, you know his fiancé Jane is with the women of the church this afternoon, having her bridal shower. I figured it would be good if the men did something for Joe." He paused, then added hastily, "I mean, not a 'shower' or anything like that, exactly, but....maybe...you know, something more for men...."

As his voice trailed off helplessly into the unknown, I knew it was time to speak.

"It's really a great idea," I encouraged. "In fact, it's such a pioneering thing that it seems like none of us really knows how to do it. I'm not really sure myself, but here's a suggestion: What if we all gathered around Joe here and those of us who are married might talk to him a bit."

Unsure, I opened my hands and lifted my shoulders, "You know, maybe about things you wish someone had told you before you got married yourself. Some things you've learned, some good surprises, even mistakes you've made that you'd like to help Joe avoid."

The host knit his brow for a moment, examined the styrofoam cup in his hand. "Well," he confessed, "you're sure right that we don't know what to do." With a sigh, he turned to the room of men. "It's worth a try."

Putting his fingers to his lips, he gave a loud whistle. "Heads up, guys!" he shouted. Like chaff before the wind, the chatter blew away before this welcome diversion. "It's great to be here together to honor our brother Joe before the wedding on Saturday. Right now, I'd like to try something—if we could all gather around him here."

A tentative shuffle, and the dozen or so men there clustered around the couch.

MARRIED MEN TALK

"Now I want the married men here to talk to Joe," the host announced. "Maybe tell him the best thing about marriage for you, some important things you've learned or wish someone had told you when you were where he is right now. Then all of us, whether you're married or not, can lay hands on Joe together and bless him."

Yes, Lord! I thought. *This is the way to do it!* Excitedly, I waited…and waited, as a deadly silence fell upon the room.

Before long, Joe's eyes dropped, embarrassed.

I panicked. *Come on, Father!* I cried out in my heart. *Don't let the men abandon our brother Joe! Kick some married guy here in the butt and make him step out!*

Moments passed, endless and empty. At last, a voice—uncertain but deliberate—broke through the darkness like a sword of light.

"Well…," one man offered hesitantly, "I'd have to say that I was a little unsure when I got married. But now that Sue and I are going on two years together, I can say that getting married was the best thing I ever did."

Alright! I thought, excitedly waiting for the man to flesh out his testimony. To my dismay, however, he sat smiling in relief, self-satisfied and eminently finished. At once, I knew that I'd have to push him for the heart of his offering.

"That's really great, Bill," I broke in. "But I wonder if you could help Joe out a bit here and be a little more specific. Just what, exactly, is so good about being married?"

Bill paused and looked off in reflection. "I guess," he said finally, turning to sweep his gaze thoughtfully around the room, "it's like a lot of the time a woman can accept you and still love you even after you mess up. I mean, a lot better somehow than you can accept and forgive yourself. It's just great to feel free to talk about things together and know it's alright, no matter what comes up."

Bold and true, Bill had slain the shame dragon and flung wide the gate. Even before he had finished, Joe was no longer perched tensely on the edge of the couch, but relaxed and sitting back, listening with appreciation.

In fact, Bill's self-satisfied smile had demonstrated that proclaiming the Father's blessings before other men strengthens and uplifts the one sharing as well. Soon all the men were anticipating their turn to speak. Several single men spoke about how Joe's bold move encouraged them in their own preparation for marriage. When all had told their stories, we closed with a rousing prayer for Joe and his coming marriage, thanking the Father for blessing us all at this bachelor party with His rich, even tasteful fellowship.

GIFT TO HIS WIFE

Later, after the wedding, Joe told me how much he appreciated the brothers' honesty and encouragement at the party. In fact, he said, it was as much a gift to his wife—that is, the gift of a man centered in God's community of men, secured in his masculine identity, confident and excited about his future with her.

Even as I enjoyed how the Father had used my suggestion for the party, I wondered: Why do so few men of God give this simple but powerful gift to each other? Why are we content to let the women have their bridal showers and receive the blessing and grace of other women who have walked the path ahead of them, while we men remain alone and afraid?

Later still, it struck me: When a woman becomes pregnant, her friends come around her with a "baby shower" to encourage and bless her with their feminine fellowship and stories of mothering. Why can't dads in the church do something similar for men on the threshold of fatherhood?

I remember when Mary told me she was pregnant. I was excited— but scared. Was I ready for this overwhelming responsibility? How would I ever make enough money to pay the doctor bills and regular life expenses for a child? The disconnect between me and my father felt suddenly deeper as I searched my experience growing up for resources to guide me as a dad myself.

Mary confided to me some fears of her own, but when the invitation to her "baby shower" came from the women of the church, she was relieved.

I was jealous.

No man ever contacted me to say, "Gordon, being a father is awesome business, and we want to come alongside you as men to give you some encouragement and support." It's enough to say that wasn't because no man in my church had ever been a father.

While the mom-to-be celebrated, the dad-to-be trembled.

Men, it's time to get real. Getting married, like becoming a father, is a momentous experience which defines your life thereafter (see *Do Pirates Wear Pajamas? and Other Mysteries in the Adventure of Fathering*). As such, it's as frightening as it is promising. We need each other alongside in order to be the husbands and fathers God intends us to be.

Heads up, Christian brothers: wedding bells are ringing, babies are kicking to come out, and men are needing each other.

Are we ready?

> **Men of the Great Depression and WWII learned to shut down emotionally and withdraw from relationship. Their sons therefore struggled to focus their unmet longing for Dad's affection.**

14

Homosexuality

and History

A Perfect Storm

See, I will send you the prophet Elijah before that
great and dreadful day of the Lord comes. He will
turn the hearts of the fathers to their children and the
hearts of the children to their fathers; or else I will
come and strike the land with a curse.
Malachi 4:5,6NIV

A PERFECT STORM IN HISTORY has devastated boys over the last century, leaving a pervasive insecurity among men today.

My own father was born during WWI in 1916. When he became a teenager in 1929 on the threshold of manhood, the stock market crashed. Thrift was not a virtue, but a necessity as he grew up. "You were lucky to have a meal on your plate in those days," as his older sister, my late aunt, once told me. "Times were tough, but we didn't complain, because everyone else was in the same boat."

To an adult, such fortitude is admirable. To a boy, however, "No costly two-cent ice cream for you!" stirs painful deprivation and shame, not noble endurance and camaraderie.

Certainly, adults can't always change historical circumstances, but they can help a child to feel understood and accepted. "I know you want an ice cream and feel disappointed," a parent might offer. "I wish we could afford it right now, but we can't." Too often, however, it's easy to shame the child simply for wanting it—as in, "You want *what*? Don't you see how much everyone else is struggling, too?"

Camaraderie may share the suffering, but doesn't eliminate it. Amid such material deprivation and emotional disregard, even heartfelt needs are remaindered—and diligently, if not ruthlessly suppressed. "The Great Depression" aptly named both the economic and the emotional scene.

ROBBED OF BOYHOOD

When my father became a young man, WWII dashed all lingering hope of honoring his heart and entertaining his own desires.

In effect, Dad's generation was robbed of both boyhood and adolescence. The exigencies of Depression and World War trumped youthful self-expression and carefree fun; external circumstance, not internal aspiration, dictated destiny (see "The Commandment to Enjoy vs. the Spirit of Deprivation" in *Religion vs Reality*).

By the time the Depression/WWII-era males became fathers, their emotionality had been truncated. They never learned to show compassion because they were never shown it, nor to honor their hearts because to do so was branded as petty if not "sissy." Since their own childhood had been precluded, often they couldn't relate to their children. As a boy, I learned to think twice before asking for a nickel ice cream. (see "One Ice Cream at a Time: Growing up with the Child's Help" in *Do Pirates Wear Pajamas?*)

Many sons of the WWII warriors lost their fathers in the war. Those whose fathers returned grew up feeling emotionally alienated from Dad and abandoned. An entire generation of boys became an emotional underclass as men.

Because divorce was so shameful then, our fathers were more likely than today to be physically present in the home. Often, however, they were not able to be emotionally present and honor the hearts of others— especially their sons', because girls were expected to be emotional.

To every boy, Dad defines masculinity. Alienation and violence—as modeled by the away-at-war soldier and undergirded in movies by the cowboy drifter—therefore defined the masculine hero for my generation.

In World War, like the Wild West, wounds are considered shameful. There's no room for "sissy" things like crying, or even love. As boys, we learned from our fathers not to face our wounds or express pain. "Stop crying!" we were commanded—then warned, "or I'll give you something to cry about." Decades later at fifty, my respect for Superman was challenged when in his new movie the Man of Steel took a second look at Lois Lane.

The lesson to postwar boys was clear: it's dangerous to be real before a man. If you express your pain, he'll increase it. Real men, in fact, are quiet if not distant; only girls express honest, heartfelt emotion. An entire generation of sons learned that it's safer to depress your emotions than to express yourself—and by definition, end up depressed (see "Depression— or Expression?" in *Religion vs. Reality*).

ABUSIVE MESSAGE

The simple but abusive message resounded in our hearts: It's unmanly to be real.

War is the devil's game. In it, the father of Lies promises to produce manhood, but in fact destroys it—if not on the battlefield, in the disallowed hearts of the soldiers. The sons of the soldiers learn from Dad to feel ashamed of their need for masculine emotional bonding, and become confused about focusing their natural longing for it.

This is the tragic legacy of war, which festers for generations after the peace treaties have been signed. A particular war may be won on the battlefield by soldiers, but all wars are lost in the hearts of their sons and daughters, who suffer as casualties from emotional abandonment (see "War and Manhood" in *Fight like a Man: A New Manhood for a New Warfare*).

In the 1960s, the sons of the WWII warriors began coming into manhood. As all sons, we longed to be men in our fathers' eyes. If Dad balks at the expressed emotion in a clear and spoken blessing, however, a son's only hope is to receive an implied blessing from Dad by being like him. We therefore struggled like Dad to repress our emotions, maintain relational distance, seek violence as a context for proving manhood, and conform to hierarchical, post-military corporate ranking. But the more we tried, the more we failed—and felt unreal.

Burdened with shame for not having the authentic stuff of manhood, we became angry at our fathers for not giving it to us and then judging us as unmanly for not having it. When Dad withdraws from his son, the boy feels not only abandoned but ashamed, as if Dad doesn't want to identify with him. In order to overcome that shame, Boomers rebelled.

Often, we sought a license to do so by identifying with scorned ethnic groups, whose economic and social oppression might better advertise our white fathers' sin and thereby, justify our anger. We hoped the nobility of minorities' suffering would rub off on ourselves and cover the shame we felt from our white heritage in Dad (see "Victory over Racism" in *Fight like a Man*).

Eventually, women blew the whistle on our charade, and their growing voice resonated with authority in the vacuum left by our distant fathers.

In the absence of winsome masculine models, that is, as boys we bonded sympathetically to Mom, who also often felt emotionally abandoned by Dad herself. Unlike him, Mom more likely *was* hospitable to our emotions. Later, as young men, we displaced this dysfunction onto women and looked to girlfriends for permission to be real—and for safety from the shame of not measuring up to Dad.

We deferred to women as mentors and tried to gain their favor by now being like them, namely, sensitive, soft, and deferential. To scorn Dad's war and emotional distance we proclaimed "Peace and Love."

We grew our hair long and scorned masculine values like strength and decisive action as "chauvinistic."

SENSITIVE BUT NOT PASSIVE

But abdicating our masculinity and trying to be feminine simply didn't work. "We wanted men to get sensitive, but we didn't want them to get passive," as one feminist friend at Stanford exclaimed to me in 1967. "What happened?" (see "Seeking the Brown Ooze" in *Sons of the Father*).

Something essential to manhood, we young men of the sixties knew, was missing from our lives. But we couldn't name it, much less attain it, simply because we had never seen it. Indeed, we felt ashamed and disloyal to Dad even for wanting it.

Try as we did, we couldn't get it from women.

Intimidated by our fathers' "Greatest Generation," nevertheless we dared not lash back at them directly. After all, these were the great war heroes, who had indeed saved civilization from "a new Dark Age," in Winston Churchill's dramatic words. We feared that if we expressed any anger directly toward our fathers, they would only give us more to cry about.

Normal adolescent rebellion therefore arrived among us laced with a crippling insecurity. The old men, who won their manhood in military battles, could not bless our manhood in peacetime. Too young for Korea, we lacked a war in which to earn their blessing.

By the time our very own war arrived in Vietnam, most of us had begun to realize that our fathers would never give us the blessing of manhood. And so we were determined to seek a manhood apart from Dad's image. The ill-conceived Vietnam war, engineered by the old men and commanded by their military draft, felt less like becoming a man and more like cow-towing to Dad—indeed, sacrificing your life to uphold a false masculinity.

Our anger soon crystallized unto hatred. "Bring the war home, kill your parents!" we cried out at protest rallies. The 1968 French student uprising cut to the chase with their chant, *Les amis de mon père sont mes ennemis!* (Friends of my father are my enemies).

Our "stop crying or else" fathers had demonstrated they could not respond compassionately to wounding, so we dared not face our longing for their love, much less confess it to them. Instead, we became creative at passive-aggressive vengeance.

Before men who would die for America on the battlefield, we burned the flag and our draft cards. Before those who predicated their manly strength upon women's weakness, we supported radical feminism. Before those who stood tall for sober, silent, and principled morality, we hailed drugs, rock 'n roll, and free sex. Before those taught to cover their shame by denigrating people of color, we affirmed Black Power. Before proud veterans, we marched for peace. Scorning our fathers' Wheaties, Chevvy sedans, and flattops, we promoted granola, old VWs, and long hair.

HIPPIES AND FATHERS

Even as a wronged boy in his powerlessness might fantasize dying in order to "make Daddy sorry," Boomer men committed gender suicide. Mercilessly, even jealously, we scorned traditional manhood and anyone who benefitted from manifesting it—from football players to Vietnam veterans. When I was a graduate student at Stanford during the 1967 anti-war protests, the football team retaliated by jumping the long-haired student body president one night and shaving his head and beard.

"The hippies were the sons of the World War Two warriors," as the late men's ministry author Dave Simmons put it succinctly.[31] The famed youth rebellion of the sixties, that is, was hosted by political and social agendas to end racism, sexism, and militarism. But it was fueled by an unfulfilled longing for Daddy—whose heart lay buried and thereby, unmoved.

Judging our fathers to be racist, sexist, and militarist, we became anxious to dissociate from the shame of their worldview and thereby, from their definition of manhood. We tried desperately to sever from our masculine roots.

As we righteously renounced Dad's soldier model of manhood, however, we found little vision among ourselves or in history to replace it. For thousands of years before us, men had based their manhood on overpowering others, most notably in making war and in subjugating women. The hippie cry for "Peace and Love" seemed our only alternative—but its logical manifestation in pacifism and feminism never seized our masculine imagination.

In the absence of a credible manly alternative, eventually our hatred of Dad became ingrown and metastasized into a hatred of all things masculine—even ourselves. Our "social revolution" was thereby co-opted by a demonic man-hating principality, clothed in "politically correct" ideology to eliminate "male aggression." Its "softer" emphasis on universalism and tolerance undermined masculine focus and initiative, and bred passivity among us (see "Out from the Womb" in *Healing the Masculine Soul*).

Certainly, the stoic determination which history required of the WWII generation enables men to persevere amid great disappointment and suffering. It names enemies, focuses energies, wins wars, and earns a nation's esteem. But it emotionally truncates and deeply wounds their sons, leaving a generation of boys with empty hearts longing for manly love and embrace.

MAN-HATING PRINCIPALITY

As so many fathers and sons in that era, this widespread "generation gap" drove my father and me painfully apart into mutual disregard if not contempt.

Naively, I had imagined that my attacks on his lifestyle and belief system would force Dad to face his "narrow-minded" perspective, confess how he had discounted and wounded me, and affirm me at last. But my harsh and shaming judgment only showed that I had become the very image of what I scorned in him—and drove us further apart.

The enemy of God and men had done his job masterfully. It took years for me to realize that I was simply using radical politics as a weapon to punish my conservative father for not giving me the love I needed.

With no other models or resources to defend myself against his judgment, I couldn't face and feel my pain openly. Even as our conflict was engineered by the father of Lies, Dad's rejection ultimately led me to lie to myself in order to cover the deep pain which flooded into my heart. *Who cares about his love anyhow?* I scoffed.

Real men know in their hearts that the father-son bond is far deeper than any rational assent—or disregard. In fact, I did care deeply about my father's love. I was devastated by his rejection. When eventually I had expended my arsenal of ideological bullets on him, I saw no option but to suppress the pain. Indeed, I locked it in my heart and tossed the key into a dark canyon of despair.

COUNTERFEIT NOURISHMENT

Even as an unwatered plant shrivels, unmitigated deprivation starves the human spirit and leaves it vulnerable to counterfeit nourishment. For such a time as this, the father of Lies has been waiting. As a deep and crippling father-wound rooted this man-hating principality among a generation of sons, its bitter fruit began thereby to manifest in a very specific and upending way.

In that season, I crashed often at a commune in the San Francisco area among hospitable friends with an empty couch. Eventually, my commune-crashing ended as the rooms filled up with more committed members, and via a newspaper ad I rented a room in a house owned by another single man. Shortly after I moved in, he cooked a lavish dinner to welcome me. To my shock, he then told me he was gay and glad I had come because he was looking for a "fresh new partner." After an uneasy sleep, the next morning I moved out and into my VW bug.

Awhile afterward, at a local peace rally, I struck up a lively exchange with an older man standing beside me. Eventually, he suggested we go back to his place and continue our conversation over a bite to eat. Soon after we arrived, he put some snack food out on the table and promptly began to proposition me.

"I...uh...I don't know...what's going on," I managed, backing away toward the door. "I mean, I appreciate your hospitality, but...I guess, like, I'd better leave." With that, I turned quickly and walked out.

On another occasion, a neighbor told me about a local bar he especially liked and invited me to go there one night for a beer. While we sat at the table, another man came up to me and handed me a note which turned out to be an offer of sex. Confused, I showed it to my neighbor, who just shrugged his shoulders knowingly. Gingerly, I got up from the table and left.

Certainly, these three incidents could have been mere coincidence in that season of "revolution" when homosexuality was drawing increasing media attention. Nevertheless, they combined to make me wonder why gay men were approaching me. While I felt no erotic draw and nothing ever went beyond my awkward retreats, a puzzling discomfort remained.

EQUIPPED FOR HEALING

Awhile later, after becoming a Christian and receiving the baptism of Holy Spirit, I felt equipped to seek healing for my childhood wounds. Through healing conferences, counseling, reading books, much prayer, and brotherly support, I began getting in touch with my anger toward my father and releasing it, like Jesus, "with loud cries and tears" before Father God (Heb. 5:7; see "Meeting the Enemy: a First Skirmish" in *No Small Snakes: A Journey into Spiritual Warfare*).

As I begged Holy Spirit to take me beneath my anger to face the pain which it masked, I felt the consuming tension between Dad and me. Determined to be healed from the awful wounds between us, at last I fell on my knees in prayer and surrendered it all to the Father of us both.

In my mind, I pictured myself standing before Dad. At once, a deep sadness overwhelmed me and my body began to shake. "Come, Lord Jesus!" I cried out desperately. "Be with me here as I try to talk to Dad!" As I sank into the fear, suddenly I began to cry—then sobbed as a voice from deep in my heart broke forth at last, "Daddy, don't leave me! Please, don't hurt me! I'm so scared of you—I just want you to love me, Daddy!"

At last, this immeasurable pain, for so long dammed up in my heart, rose up and burst out of me like a flood. After awhile, my crying ebbed and a peace settled over me. I sighed deeply. For so many years I had lied to myself, saying that I didn't need my father's love. But now my very body itself had revealed that denial as a cowardly cover-up.

In fact, I experienced in that moment what Jesus promised: "You will know the truth, and the truth will set you free" (John 8:32).

Eventually, as I allowed myself to feel my longing for Dad's love, the simple text, "God is love" came to mind (1 John 4:8). At that, I realized that any love I might have wanted or received from my father would have come *from* God and only *through* Dad. So I determined to go to the

Source for it (see "Go to the Source for Love" in *Healing the Masculine Soul*).

"Father God, I need your love!" I declared. "Please, Father, pour out your love on me!" That openness at last to Father God for lost father-love from Dad opened the floodgates yet again. Again I wept, but this time my tears turned to joy when I sensed His love filling me for the first time (see "To Know the Father" in *Healing the Masculine Soul*).

The tears which older men had warned would make me a "sissy," in fact made me a real man—that is, a man truly real, even a son of the Father at last (see "Weeping Warrior" in *Fight like a Man*).

ROOT OF PAIN

Expressing this crippling pain freely in the presence of Jesus, I no longer needed to fear and repress it. In fact, as I prayed further, I asked God to take me to its root and show me my father as He saw Dad.

In that moment, I remembered stories Dad had told me of his being beaten and bruised as a boy and young man by his own father—an illiterate factory worker who had been forced to leave school after second grade to work sixty hours a week in the local fabric mill. Though Dad had never beaten me, his pent-up anger often frightened me. Yet again, I burst out into tears—this time not only for my wounds, but for my father's wounds and for his father's as well (see "Roots and Fruits" in *Do Pirates Wear Pajamas?*).

A little boy, I realized, cries *from* his father's wounds; Daddy hits or shames you and you cry. But a real man cries *for* his father's wounds, as an intercessor, willing to feel Dad's wounds and bear them to Jesus even as He on the cross. In fact, if you don't cry *from* your father's wounds, if you bottle up the pain inside, you can't cry *for* him because you'll never see his brokenness that caused him to wound you. Your heart won't be moved to forgive him genuinely, and you'll carry around the wound and its bitterness. Worse, that spirit of judgment which set you against each other will rise up yet again in the next generation to set you against your own children.

"Whatever you don't forgive your father for, you'll do to your son," as one 80-year-old brother declared poignantly at one of my men's conferences.

As I wept for Dad's awful boyhood pain from his own father, I saw how my bitterness toward him had only consumed my best energies and distracted me from what Father God wanted to do in my life. The resentment and hatred no longer felt strong, but only destructive—and I wanted no more of it.

"In the name of Jesus, I forgive you, Dad," I spoke out loud, "for not respecting my heart, for punishing me instead of holding me, for making me ashamed of my feelings and afraid to be a man."

At last, it was time to release my hatred of Dad. I set the cross between me and Dad, between him and his father, and on back through generations of Dalbey men who had hated their fathers. Asking for the blood of Jesus to cover me, I then renounced the man-hating spirit which had for so long distracted me and my forefathers from Father God's purposes, and took authority over it at last:

"In the name of Jesus, I bind you man-hating spirit and cast you out and away from me and into the hands of Jesus. I ask for the supernatural blood of Jesus to cleanse the natural Dalbey bloodline in me of this evil spirit. Replace it, Father God, with your Holy Spirit. Give me a joy in my masculinity that is Your joy in me as your son!" As I prayed further, additional spirits surfaced—including shame, abandonment, alienation, anger, victim, passivity, and unworthiness—and I cast them out as well.

Soon I could let go to Father God any right or desire to punish my father for hurting me. In fact, I released to Jesus all hope of ever receiving from Dad what I needed from him, acknowledged Father God as my true Father, and asked Him to give me what my earthly dad could not. Finally, I asked God to place a "hedge of thorns" around me to keep me on track with His purposes (see Hosea 2:6).

UNEXPECTED BLESSING

An unexpected blessing emerged through this process. The more I saw Dad with Jesus' eyes, the more I recognized his many admirable character traits. This allowed me to identify with Dad as a man and to honor my heart as a son. Ultimately, it led me genuinely to honor him—and as I did, to feel affirmed in my manly heritage (see "Hippies, Fathers, and Forgiveness," in Sons of the Father).

Eventually, I visited Dad and asked him to forgive me for dishonoring and shaming him in the past. Thankfully, he did. In the maturity of surrendering myself thereby to Father God, I stopped demanding like a child that Dad give me what I needed, and went instead like a man to Father God to ask for it. Thereafter, I could accept and affirm Dad for who he was, honor and give to him out of my heart, and receive the blessings of his heritage as my own. In that blessing, we enjoyed our final years together.

Through this process, I sensed at last why gay men had approached me, precisely amid my father's rejection. Suppressing my internal cry for Dad's love had not dispelled that awful pain, but only compressed and pressurized it in my heart to "broadcast" silently. The other men had allowed their own wound to lead them into suppressing their manhood unto practicing homosexuality. They were picking up on my signal, and responding to it out of their own brokenness (see "Kick Me Spirits" in *No Small Snakes*).

It's not natural for a boy to hate his father. But when it's too painful to stay open and vulnerable to Daddy, his spirit cries out for reinforcements to fabricate strength and block off that pain. The father of Lies is happy to oblige with a *super*natural spirit of anger—as a teaser.

Even as a small dose of addictive substance gives you a high at first but can only be maintained with a larger dose, the enemy eventually prescribed a spirit of hatred to "protect" me from being wounded further by Dad. Since that spirit was already in my bloodline via Dad and his own father, it felt altogether familiar and I bought it. (see "Homosexuality and the Father-Wound: Outing the Man-Hating Spirit" in *Religion vs. Reality*)

Thus, my deep unresolved anger at my father had beckoned a man-hating spirit to cut me off from him and subconsciously, I had welcomed it within me. Once resident, however, the demon led me to hate not only Dad, but to reject masculinity. Thus, the politically correct 1960's culture, unto today. Other men with a man-hating spirit from their own father-wound received my distress signal and were drawn toward me by that "familiar spirit" in us both.

While I never had any erotic attraction to other men, my natural impulse to defend against the shame of that implication hooked me into the enemy's game. When at last I had faced and wept for my father-wound, I saw that efforts to deny my wound were only handing it over to the prince of Darkness and clouding the truth that would set me free from its pain.

ENEMY'S STRATAGEM

At last, I saw the enemy's stratagem. To a generation of fatherless men, he charges, "You want another man's love and touch!" Overwhelmed by the fear of being homosexual and reeling from its shame, men deny that charge and barricade against each other—which only prompts a deeper, compulsive longing to bond with another man.

And so, men swallow the father of Lies' bait. In fact, it's true: Every man *does* want another man's love and embrace—not, however, from just any other man, and not sexually, but specifically and altogether normally from Dad.

When a naturally flowing stream becomes dammed up with storm debris, it eventually bursts to flood and destroy the terrain. Similarly, when the natural longing of a boy for his daddy's love and affection is discounted or squelched, it can build up and eventually burst to misfocus sexually on other men (see "Lost among Men: A non-Political View of Homosexuality" in *Healing the Masculine Soul*).

Thus, I saw the blessing of my literally crying out this wholly natural and God-ordained need in every boy. In doing so, I re-connected at last with my authentic self—and pre-empted the father of Lies.

In the light of this truth, I saw the masterful deception in the enemy's accusation that any challenge to the homosexual agenda is "homophobic" and therefore, invalid. Indeed, most men today *are* homophobic—because the father-wound which fuels homosexuality has become so widespread that we're all vastly susceptible. "An old person shakes at the mention of bones," as the Nigerian Igbo proverb from my Peace Corps village puts it.

The enemy of God revels as men today do for him this work of hating manhood—either by falling to homosexuality or scorning other men who manifest it. Father God's ministry to men, meanwhile, is not about hating homosexuals, but about revealing His heart—and power— to heal His sons.

In my ministry today, I simply want to draw all men away from the father of Lies and into the arms of Jesus, where Father God can demonstrate His love and re-center us in His authentic manhood. I want men to see gender confusion as stirred by the enemy of God to undermine manhood, consume our good energies, and thereby distract from our true Father's call. From that foundation, later remnant fears can be dismissed, or in fact, used to prompt a deeper healing by taking them to Jesus.

I had cried out my father-wound, forgiven Dad, cast out the demons which leveraged it, and turned to Father God at last for the father-love I needed. My formerly pent-up longing for masculine love was now acknowledged openly and focused appropriately. I was never again approached by a homosexual man.

Since I never fell into same-sex attraction myself, I can't present my experience or conclusions as definitive. Nevertheless, my story here and ministry to men around the world for decades have convinced me that homosexuality is most often rooted in a deep father-wound, and that's why it's growing so fast in this increasingly fatherless world. I therefore submit my historical scenario and personal story as evidence worth considering for men who want to overcome sexual brokenness and are willing to be as real as that process requires.

> To control sexual desire, religion reduces it to a manageable form in morality, thereby divorcing it from spirituality and enforcing compliance with shame.

15

Sexuality & Religion

A Marriage Made in Hell

When Christ died, he took that entire rule-dominated way of life down with him and left it in the tomb, leaving you free to "marry" a resurrection life and bear "offspring" of faith for God....
Rom. 7:4TMB

The Law brings death, but the Spirit brings life.
2 Corinth. 3:6

I'VE TRIED HEREIN TO PORTRAY the roots of sexual desire and its fulfillment in marriage. Like marriage, that fulfillment is not about measuring up to a standard of thought or moral behavior, but rather, an ongoing process of learning to trust God and surrender to His purposes. I've noted that the Father's plan for sexuality is often sabotaged by efforts to cover shame and seize righteousness via our human performance—as in religion.

In fact, an "immoral" act commonly refers to a sexual misdeed. Malevolence such as murder, warmaking, racism, or disregard for the poor we might label as irresponsible, harmful, unethical, even evil—but rarely immoral. This shotgun marriage of sex and morality reflects the spiritual bankruptcy of our secular worldview, in which an "immoral" act bears no intrinsic consequence, but rather, merely violates culturally accepted norms and is thereby enforced by shame.

Presumptuously, we hijack sexuality from its supernatural home in the realm of spiritual power, and domesticate it to serve our own natural desires. We regard sexual desire like language, in which words have meaning only insofar as the people who speak it attribute that meaning. We feel free to use the words or sexual acts however we please, adapting them at will to fit our culture or era.

As I've portrayed in my other books, our secular society today cannot believe in God's power nor trust Him to wield it for our good. Among us, religion has therefore co-opted spirituality in order to fabricate a sense of control. Its counterpart morality is often defined and upheld by a list of proscribed sexual activity.

As Mary has noted in her chapter, however, the joy in fullness of sexual expression lies in letting go of control—which requires protective boundaries in order to do safely.

Morality is about what we don't do, and is upheld largely by the fearful shame in doing it. Sexual fulfillment, however, is about what God does. It's upheld by the demonstrated love and power of the One who created us male and female in His image.

SANCTIFIED MORALITY

To the world—and often to Christians—religion is simply a sanctified morality. It's about what we do for God, not what God has done for us in Jesus. Religion thereby excludes Jesus and His saving work in our behalf. Ultimately, it degenerates into a synthetic righteousness in which we look to religion for the measure of success, but discount Jesus as the means.

"Many approach the teachings of Jesus as just another form of the Law," as one pastor draws the line between religion and grace:

> To most He just brought a new set of rules. Grace is different from the Law in that the favor comes before the obedience. Under grace the commandments of the Lord come fully equipped with the ability to perform them...to those who hear from the heart. Grace enables what it commands.[32]

Instead of receiving the Father's forgiveness to rekindle our hearts, His grace in Jesus to persevere against our sin-nature, and His power in Holy Spirit to fulfill His call, we end up seizing control ourselves via a "rule-dominated way of life," as Paul warned in the opening Scripture. We urge religious laws, moral codes, and behavior standards, which presumably confer Father God's favor upon those who work hard enough to abide them.

In order to fabricate a sense of control, religion therefore denies the simple fact that in our natural human effort we're not able to keep God's Laws (see Rom. 7:18). In fact, that's why Jesus came: to empower us to do what's best for us. Religion therefore preempts the saving work of Jesus and denies God's power at work among us.

Eventually, the insecurity from that lie denies the spiritual essence of sexuality and reduces it to a manageable form in moral behavior standards. Thus, the seductive Tree of the Knowledge of Good and Evil. Religion is about what we do to save ourselves and is predicated on a master's commandment to obey. Jesus, however, is about what God does to save us and bears a Father's invitation to trust. Thus, the liberating Tree of Life (see "From Obedience to Trust: Slavery or Sonship?" in *Religion vs. Reality*).

To confine the spiritual expanse of sexual desire to mere behavior standards is like caging a lion. This wild and powerful creature looks out through steel bars at a world of freedom, longing to be released back into its authentic home. Forced to depend upon its captors and live on humanly prepared meat, the lion must forget its root origins, deny its own integrity, and submit to a false, imposed reality. Eventually, it becomes passive, forsakes its roar, and capitulates its identity (see "When the Lion Roars" in *Healing the Masculine Soul*).

CAGE OF SHAME

Similarly, human beings were not designed for cages. With its bars of shame, religion is the cage which denies us freedom and fullness of life in the Father. Like a humanly designed cell, religion offers apparent safety and the sustenance of acceptance in exchange for reality and the freedom to embrace it. As Mark Twain observed, "religion is a set of things which the average man thinks he believes and wishes he was certain."[33]

Forbidden to be real upon pain of shame and rejection, we become enslaved to religion and take refuge in compliance, striving to be right. Our sin-nature, however, makes that goal impossible. In order to deny the reality of our hopelessness, in fact, we must deny the Savior who delivers us from it. Ultimately, we anaesthetize the Father's Spirit, who otherwise roars in our hearts not only to conquer the enemy but to bond sexually—even in His image.

Religion is a turn-off.

Jesus, meanwhile, restores men and women to our created destiny as sons and daughters of the Father—and thereby, sparks and blesses desire between a man and woman surrendered to Him.

Granted, our sin-nature requires us to be reminded of God's boundaries. "I have not come to abolish (the law and the prophets)," as Jesus declared, "but to fulfill them" with His presence and power (Matt. 5:17). When a child is holding his/her father's hand, that is, there's no need for fences.[34] Authentic sexual expression, therefore, is not about being properly restrained by your willpower, but being faithfully led by Father God's hand.

What's more, in the Father's hand we're free to experience sexual desire because we know He's present to focus it in our very best interest. Without that freedom—caged by shame—we feed on counterfeit, humanly fabricated sexuality, from quick hook-ups to pornography. Those who deny and repress their genuine desires the most rigidly are often those who succumb to such false "satisfaction" the most deeply.

Among youth, eventually an angry sense of betrayal arises, that religion and cultural morality have lied to them and withheld the best. All too often, the children of religious families bear this resentment and rebel when they're old enough to climb over the fence.

AUTHENTIC FREEDOM

They see through the pretenses of their elders' religion and reject its shame. Their very bodies long for authentic freedom. Denied and wounded by Christianity, too often they turn from God and misfocus their desire on the world. Hence, the spirit of license, the counterfeit freedom hosted by the father of Lies. The twin offspring of religion are the polarities of compliant bondage and rebellious licentiousness.

Thankfully, the Father of Truth has not abandoned us in this our eternal predicament. In fact, as Paul declared, Jesus "took that entire rule-dominated way of life down with him and left it in the tomb, leaving you free to 'marry' a resurrection life and bear 'offspring' of faith for God" (Rom. 7:4TMB).

Spirituality and sexuality, that is, are like marriage partners. When united together according to the Father's will, they produce neither stoic slaves nor angry rebels, but authentic sons and daughters who enjoy their sexuality as intended within the Father's protective boundaries.

Spirituality and religion, on the other hand, are like an arranged marriage, perpetrated by the powers of the world as for political convenience to serve the kingdom of this world. It's easier to proclaim righteous standards of sexual behavior than to confess you can't meet them—and trust God to empower you to meet them.

Religion, that is, has infected sexuality with shame by divorcing it from spirituality and bonding it unnaturally to morality. It compels us to control desire rather than trust Father God to mediate it. This fear reflects the sad fact that we don't want the sexual fulfillment God offers us as badly as we want to cover our shame. The enemy of God and humanity secures this fear by distracting us from Jesus, who has already dealt with our shame on the cross.

Thus separated from God-who-is-love, religion separates love from sexuality and fosters counterfeits. Caged and cut off from its genuine roots we forget where sexual desire comes from and its created purpose. Lacking that sense of foundational truth, we become vulnerable to the world's many seductive, counterfeit sexual expressions designed by the father of Lies.

SIN-HUNGRY CREATURES?

To religion, in fact, human beings are wild, sin-hungry creatures who must be captured by threat of punishment and caged by shame. At the other, universalist polarity, to the world we're lovely, self-actualizing creatures with only wonderful desires that must be freely and tolerantly expressed.

We're not defined, however, by the spirit of religion or the spirit of this world's universalism, but rather, by Father God—to whom we're neither of these extreme, even destructive identities. Rather, we're His beloved children created to express His love freely—even as we're bound by our fallen nature which would misfocus and sabotage that freedom.

In the Bible, God has graciously revealed to His sons and daughters the boundaries within which that freedom can be safely exercised. What's more, apart from either vengeful punishment or freewheeling tolerance, the Father has sent Jesus to break the chains of our sin-nature, receive His Spirit, and enable us to abide those boundaries to fulfill His blessing of sexuality.

Self-control, after all, is a fruit of the Spirit (Gal. 5:23). It's not the natural result of your effort, but the super-natural result of God's effort.

Because it's not natural for us fallen human beings to let go of control, even to God, marriage can always be fearful to some extent. In fact, you can only let go of controlling others insofar as you're securely surrendered to the Father's control. Husbands and wives therefore never finish the process of surrendering to God and each other. The more you trust God, the more He trusts you and therefore leads you into greater adventures together for His Kingdom—which in turn require deeper trust in Him and each other.

JOURNEY OF RELATIONSHIP

The gift of learning, that is, bears the responsibility to walk out its lessons. Trusting God—even to uphold your marriage—is not an end in itself, if only because we never fully get there as long as we're clothed in human flesh. Trust is a process that happens along the journey of relationship.

It's not about trusting Father God to bring about your desired outcome, but rather, to be Himself—that is, to use your desires to draw you to Himself and lead you into His good purposes. When you don't "get what you want," that relationship with God allows you to believe He'll bring about something better for you later.

It's called faith.

What's more, God has an agenda far greater than your marriage, namely, to establish His Kingdom rule "on earth as it is in heaven" (Luke 11:2). Being "suitable companions" means joining God together in that task, in the role He's designed for your marriage. If you don't know your calling, He's not playing hide and seek. Kneel at the foot of your bed together and ask Him. Moving in the flow of God's Spirit draws you closer to Him—and allows Him to draw you closer to each other.

That's what the fears and conflicts between a husband and wife are about, namely, training whereby you learn the character and power of God via surrendering to His overcoming love. Even as the most seasoned warriors are sent to the most significant battles, the most vital marriages are therefore marked by a desire not only to serve each other, but together to serve others, "using the same help that we ourselves have received from God" (2 Corinth. 1:5).

Truth focuses on uncovering reality. Therefore, it often stirs shame among us human beings, who are infected with a sin-nature which we're desperate to hide. Like scared children, we fear being discovered and punished (see "Blackmailed by Shame" in *Broken by Religion, Healed by God*).

In order to stand in the truth long enough to embrace its benefit, you need to feel safe. You need assurance that the bearer of truth has the compassion not only to forgive, but to bless the one otherwise condemned.

That's called grace.

That's Jesus on the cross.

The solution to a marital problem, therefore, is not winning the argument but gaining a deeper humility before God and each other. You can get there by renouncing your need to be right and the urge to justify and validate your position. On that sure and mutual foundation, you can then beg God together to reveal His position—and for enough trust in Him to be real with Him and each other.

While men are certainly capable of such unconditional love, its acceptance and compassion are archetypically modeled by that of a mother for her child. In fact, as in a nursing mother, unfettered affection and unmerited grace are largely regarded as intrinsic to femininity.

"God gave the Law through Moses," as John declared, "but grace and truth came through Jesus Christ" (John 1:17). At its worst, religion speaks truth without the grace which enables you to hear it—which makes the hearer prone to reject the truth along with the speaker. Thus, religion reflects the condemning mind of the Accuser, even the father of Lies. Above all, religion therefore fears grace, which undermines its very foundation by enabling people to face the truth—especially that of their own contrived righteousness.

Insofar as the woman bears grace, therefore, religion fears feminity.

RELIGION AND SEXISM

In order to prop up its righteous facade, religion eventually requires hierarchy to determine who's most certified to hide unquestioned from the truth about their sin nature. Between men and women, this "I'm OK, you're not OK" mentality breeds sexism, which relegates one gender to an inferior status—most often, women.

Regardless of its apparent righteousness, a position that denigrates and wounds His children—even half the human population who together with the other half comprise His very image—surely has no credibility in the Father's eyes (see "'Male Headship' and Battling for the Woman" in *Fight like a Man*). Men who denigrate women in order to hide the shame of their own inadequacy are not sons of the God revealed in Jesus, simply because they have not received the freedom from shame which Jesus died to give them (see Rom. 8:1).

Religion is toxic to women, and thereby, to sexual relationships.

Faithful and fulfilling sexual expression takes place in marriage between a man and woman who love and respect each other. Only Father God, who created the wondrous mystery of desire, can engender that. He does so for those who choose to surrender neither to the judgment of religion nor the license of this world, but to Him.

> **Love is not a goal to be achieved, but a blessing to be received.**

16

Sexuality and Spirituality

A Marriage Made in Heaven

Everyone who loves is born of God and experiences a relationship with God. The person who refuses to love doesn't know the first thing about love, because God is love. 1 John 4:16TMB

ASKING MARY TO MARRY ME, as described in Chapter 3, unleashed a host of old fears from past relationship wounds. Striving unsuccessfully to conquer those fears and "do it right," I began to feel ashamed and inadequate to the task.

It was clear to me and all my closest friends that Mary was the "suitable companion" I had prayed for so long. I wanted desperately to make our relationship work. Yet the harder I struggled to measure up to my standard of courage and integrity, the more I failed and thereby, only generated more shame and fear. Eventually, I went to a Christian therapist for counseling.

After praying on an hour-long freeway drive, I walked into his office and we reached out to shake hands. Before I could say anything, however, a single word leapt from his mouth.

"Religion!" he exclaimed—and then drew back in surprise at his own outburst.

"Uh…, well, it's…it's good to meet you," I managed.

For a moment, we stood awkwardly before each other, until finally, we gathered ourselves and sat down.

"That's really strange," he allowed. "As soon as you walked in the door, the word 'religion' just jumped out!"

Raising my eyebrows inquisitively, I hesitated. "So…, what do you make of that?"

"It does feel like the Lord," he mused, puzzled and shaking his head in amazement. After a minute, he sighed, uncertain. "Well," he ventured, "the spirit of religion is about not trusting God—like struggling to measure up to some impossibly high standard in your own strength and feeling ashamed that you're not making it. Would that in any way describe your situation?"

I smiled at last in wonder and praise. "Looks like I came to the right place!" I said.

The Father had clearly called Mary and me to minister together as seasoned warriors for His Kingdom. The enemy was therefore determined to sabotage our relationship. The Accuser's tried-and-true weapon of destruction is shame. It's an age-old tactic, which makes you desperate to defend yourself—which makes you sink deeper into lies. In this case, he cut to the core of my manhood with the charge, "Your fear shows that you don't have what it takes to be the man and husband you should be!"

He was right.

The devil may be the father of Lies, but he can speak the truth when it cuts deeply. Unlike Jesus, however, the Accuser doesn't provide the grace which allows you to face the truth and overcome its consequences.

Clearly, I didn't trust the Father's grace, and covered my lack of faith by pretending that my own efforts would compensate. The more I failed, the more I feared exposure, panicked, and pushed myself to strive harder—which perpetuated this vicious cycle.

In my fear of not measuring up, I became desperate to win God's favor—not to mention that of Mary. Instead of trusting the Father's work in me and His timing, I struggled instead to make myself love her.

The truth is, I really didn't know what love is, much less how to give it. I had therefore grasped after moral achievement standards as a more manageable substitute. That's how religion often takes root.

NATURAL LIMITATIONS

Granted, a desire to do the right thing is better than a desire to do the wrong or evil thing. But good intentions can lead to despair without honestly facing up to your natural limitations. A religious desperation to be right often overshadows a humble desire to be a real—and sabotages the mutually trusting, heartfelt relationship where love roots and grows.

If you don't have the Spirit, you'd better have the Law. But if Law is all you have, you'll never know love. "The Law brings death," as Paul noted, "but the Spirit brings life" (2Corinth. 3:6).

As the Snake knew well, The Tree of the Knowledge of Good and Evil—that is, religion—bears the devil's fruit in shame and mutual distrust. But the Tree of Life—that is, Jesus—bears the fruit of God's Holy Spirit in love (Gal. 5:22).

The performance demands of religion, that is, cast love as a commandment to be obeyed. To Father God, however, love is primarily not a goal to be achieved, but a blessing to be received. In fact, "God is love" and therefore "love comes from God," not from ourselves (1John 4: 16, 7). If you want love to give, you need to go to the Source and get it—that is, to fall on your knees and cry out, "Father, I need your love!"

True, God commands us to "love your neighbor as you love yourself" and even to "love the Lord your God with all your heart, with all your soul, and with all your strength" (Lev. 19:18, Deut. 6:5). But where are we supposed to get that love to give others and Him? He certainly knows that we can't generate love out of our sin-laden human hearts, but that we must draw close to Him in order to receive love, even to give it back to Him.

What's more, you can't make love happen, simply because you can't manipulate God to do what you want. Yet that ruse is precisely what animates religion, namely, bribing God with your righteous achievements/

sacrifices in order to earn His love and ostensibly remove your shame. The demonic deception here—if not tragic misconception—is that God has already done that in sending Jesus to die for our sins. Ironically, that's how religion becomes a distraction from Jesus—and thereby, a recipe for burnout.

FEAR OF MISTAKE

The fear of making a mistake—and paying the consequences—is the hallmark of religion. It stems from denying your sin-nature, which insures that you *will* make many mistakes. It metastacizes in a false image of the Father, as a punishing taskmaster—which kept me from celebrating His gift to me in Mary. When the Accuser charged, "You don't measure up as a man," I caved in to the logical conclusion, "Since you don't have the love and strength of character to follow through on what marriage requires, you can't get married."

The more I tried to ignore or suppress my fear of inadequacy, therefore, the more marriage threatened failure instead of promised fulfillment. My unwillingness to trust God to finish the work he started between Mary and me thereby gave the spirit of religion rein to intimidate me (see Phil. 1:6).

The simple antidote to the enemy's poison here would have been to face the truth squarely, instead of biting religion's bait of shame. "You're absolutely right, Satan," I could've said. "I don't measure up as a man or husband. Thanks for reminding me. I'm going straightaway to my Father to get what I need.

"It's clear to me He's heard my cry for a suitable companion and called Mary and me together. So I trust Him to give me what I need to be the husband she needs and I want to be."

In the world's economy, not having what you need for the job is the end of your story. In the Kingdom of God—that is, where the Father rules—it's the authentic beginning of His story, because it drives you at last to go to Him and get what you need to walk it out.

That honesty and trust in the Father would have unmasked the enemy's ruse from the get-go and released me from religion's cage of shame. I could've avoided so many fear-laden days, sleepless nights, and upset stomachs with that simple surrender. "Make friends quickly with your accuser, while you are going with him to court," as Jesus warned, "lest your accuser hand you over to the judge, and the judge to his guard, and you be put in prison" (Matt. 5:25RSV).

A farmer can plant a seed, then water, fertilize, and protect it. But only God can make the plant grow—in His season and timing (see Mark 4:28). Farming requires as much labor in faith as in the field. As Paul compared his ministry to farming, "I planted the seed, Apollos watered the plant, but it was God who made the plant grow" (1 Corinth. 3:6).

Similarly, the Father had planted His seed of love between Mary and me as an invitation to let Him develop it. I needed to water it—that is, to face my wounds, seek His healing and deliverance, marshal my prayer partners, recognize Him via His Word in the Bible, stay physically healthy, and pray. After doing my best at that, my job was simply to trust the Father to grow His love within us, in His season/timing.

In my life, however, I had not learned to trust either others or myself—so I didn't know how to stop striving and let go to Father God. My work was short-circuiting His work.

Significantly, my decision to ask Mary to marry me was not driven by religion. It was not generated solely by supernatural revelation nor motivated by either obedience or fear of punishment. Indeed, the Father confirmed His calling by giving me a reassurance in her faithfulness to Him; a strong physical attraction to her beauty; admiration for her perseverance and trustworthy character; respect for her intelligence, wisdom, and accomplishments; joy in her sense of humor; freedom in her tell-it-like-it-is, down-to-earth freshness—the list goes on far beyond the scope of this chapter, but I'll close here last but certainly not least, appreciation for the openness of her heart.

What's more, we were both Spirit-filled believers and church leaders. Mary was a psychologist and I had been a pastor. Each of us had suffered relationship wounds both as children and adults, had worked hard on our own emotional/spiritual issues, and were committed to help others similarly. Both of us were on the same page politically, spoke Spanish, had strong cross-cultural sensibilities, were highly educated, wanted to have children, and liked dancing—70's funk preferred.

Sure, we have enough differences to keep us on our knees together. In any case, from a purely natural view, we were eminently compatible and headed in the same direction.

DESPERATE TO MEASURE UP

I note this "whole" picture here because the fear and shame generated by religious performance standards can make you desperate to measure up—especially if as a child your own desires were not acknowledged and respected. In the grip of religion, it's tempting to dismiss and bypass the natural realities which are often more credible indicators of God's will. Religion can delude you into thinking, "I don't really need to know the other person; I just have to obey God and that will avoid the uncomfortable details of genuine, give-and-take relationship" (see "From Obedience to Trust: Slavery or Sonship?" in *Religion vs. Reality*).

Yet often it's precisely those realities and uncomfortable details which keep you crying out to God—and thereby, learning to know both Him and each other.

What if, indeed—as most often in this fallen world—you're not always sure what God is saying? What if you *are* sure, but can't do what He says? What if the harder you try, the more convincingly you fail? What if your heart cries out, like the Apostle Paul, "Who will save me from this body that is taking me to death?" (Rom. 7:24).

Then you're ready at last to ditch the shame of religion for the grace of relationship with your true Father—and the love of another person. You're ready, in fact, to discover like Paul, "Thanks be to *God, who does this through our Lord Jesus Christ*"—not through your frantic efforts (Rom. 7:25, italics mine).

Mary told me, for example, about a pastor she once heard preach on choosing a marriage partner. "I married my wife because God told me to!" he proclaimed righteously.

Mary shook her head in dismay. "You could almost hear the women in the congregation groan!"

It's important, of course, to believe God is working in your relationship. But this primary reference to religious duty and obedience over heartfelt love and longing for the other, wounded the feminine souls of the women there. Only the demon of religion could so mislead a man to marginalize the natural reality of his wife's beauty, character, and heart. Such distrust of God and your own heart stirs shame, with its fear of self-exposure—and thereby, a readiness to whitewash it with religion.

ORDINARY CONFIRMATION

Sure, it's important to seek God's will for your future mate. But we're not His slaves. We're His sons and daughters. The Father reveals His will for a man and woman in many ways, which most often include honoring their natural human affections and compatibility. Without that "ordinary" confirmation, when doubts and conflict arise you're likely to disengage and hide in religion—wielding judgment, condemnation, and "Bible bullets" to solidify your own position.

I'm therefore dismayed while counseling Christian couples how often I hear a husband or wife charge the spouse with some religious peccadillo like "she's not into the Word" or "he doesn't go to church every week." Criticizing your spouse's religious performance is most often a red herring designed to deflect the Spirit's "double-edged" sword of truth away from yourself (Heb. 4:12). In fact, it suggests strongly that a spirit of religion in you is a major factor in your marriage conflict.

Certainly, Mary and I are different in many ways, and that "edge" has often spurred both conflict and adventure. "If you're both the same, one of you is unnecessary," as another has wisely said. Indeed, in bringing us together, God jarred both of us out of our comfort zones graphically and forced us instead to depend upon Him for our future together.

On psychological tests, in fact, we come out exact opposites. Mary—well-trained as an organizer with attention to detail from her days as a nurse—values observations, facts, and closure. As a writer and spiritual warrior, I lean more on intuition, supernatural revelation, and "let's see where this goes" experimentation.

The fear of not measuring up as a man, however, pre-empted my customary open-ended approach. Grasping after control, I begged God for His definitive Yes or No regarding our relationship—to no avail. I panicked as my prayers for God's will and decisive guidance were met with silence.

LARGER GOAL

The Father, however, had a larger goal beyond just confirming His call to Mary and me. He wanted to seal His relationship with each of us, so we could depend on Him to seal our relationship with each other.

Once, when praying with my prayer partner, I cried out desperately, "I just want to do your will, Father! Is Mary the right one for me?"

It sounds so righteous. But in my fear of making a mistake, I heard nothing—because the Father was weaning me away from the slavery of religion into the freedom of sonship (see Rom. 8:14-16).

My friend was quiet for a minute. "I didn't get an answer," he said finally. "In fact, I got a question. I think the Lord is asking you, 'Gordon, what do *you* want?'"

That simple question startled and upended me, because I had not often heard it growing up and therefore had not learned to honor my own desires. Not trusting my heart, my internal feelings naturally short-circuited to objective standards and external requirements—the breeding ground for religion when not balanced by heartfelt desire.

In fact, I couldn't even *know* what I wanted, because I had so long suppressed the pain from not getting it. Even if I could know, I didn't believe anyone would give it to me.

I learned this in my mid-twenties, when a woman whom I had hurt confronted me. "Don't you have any feelings at all?" she demanded, exasperated. Gathering herself as a hint of grace bid for a voice, she knit her brow and asked me, "When did you cry last?"

I couldn't answer that question. Which, of course, answered her first question: No. In fact, I had few recognizable feelings beyond fear, and I had worked hard to suppress even that. I'd been trying so hard to be right that I couldn't remember when I was last real.

There's a feeling for that. It's called "sad."

Disconnected from my heart, lacking confidence in my emotional responses, I had nothing to gauge my decisions beyond what I *should* feel and *should* do. Such emotional deprivation left me vulnerable and afraid that I would betray myself, especially in relationships. Instead of seeking healing to reconnect with my heart, I baptized my fearful disengagement with religion. "I'm OK, because I want to do the *right* thing," I could say. But this religious shibboleth only hid my wound and the shame of being unable to access the *real* thing.

HUNGER FOR GOD

Thus, Carol Wimber, wife of the late John Wimber of the Vineyard churches, describes how God surprised her while begging Him to heal their church. "I had gone to God asking him what was wrong with the church, and he was showing me what was wrong with me." This forced her to her knees for days of fasting and repentance. "Out of this terrible crucible of guilt and sorrow a desperate longing for God emerged. This hunger was not for his will, it was for God himself."[36]

Thus, a heartfelt longing for relationship trumps religion's fear of not measuring up.

Ironically, my determination after "righteous" certainty only revealed my lack of faith in Father God. Worse, however, it beckoned occult demons of divination from the father of Lies—who leveraged my wound by basically telling me that Father God had abandoned me. In fact, God was simply using my uncertainty to teach me a deeper trust in Him, which Mary and I would need later as companions in His ministry together (see "Seeking God's Will, Trusting His Love" in *Sons of the Father*).

Meanwhile, I didn't want to burden Mary with all my fears, much less reveal them and appear weak. Nevertheless, she sensed this struggle in me. When I would tell her, "I love you," wisely she would ask me, "Why? What do you love about me?" That helped to bring me out of my disengaged fear zone down to earth where I could see her more clearly and offer my heart a credible case for opening up.

Still, that simple question, "What do *you* want, Gordon?" came back to upend me many times in that season. Eventually, I realized that I was begging Father God to tell me what He wanted because I didn't either trust Him to listen to what I wanted or was too disconnected to say what I genuinely wanted.

In my fear and shame, it never occurred to me that He already knew what I wanted, because He had given me the desires of my heart for Mary (Psalm 37:4). As a good Father in behalf of His daughter, He was determined to know if I wanted her badly enough to fight for her—even against my own fears.

HONOR YOUR DESIRE

"I can't believe how good Mary is," I declared at one point with the counselor.

"No," he countered. "Your problem is that you can't believe how good your Father is. You can't believe He would love you so much as to honor your desire as His son and give you something you want so much" (see "The Commandment to Enjoy vs the Spirit of Deprivation" in *Religion vs. Reality*).

Eventually, I began to surrender control to the Father and trust His love for me. In that faith, I no longer needed to love Mary in order to satisfy a religious standard of integrity and stand by my commitment to marry her. Instead, His love for Mary could filter through the crack in my emotional wall and enter my heart, to where I genuinely *wanted* to marry her—not out of duty, but out of desire.

In that process, the fear of making a mistake began to dissipate. At last, I could enjoy Mary—and realized that my desperate prayer, "God, show me your will!" reflected not my righteous faith in Him, but precisely my lack of it.

Sharing in the Father's love for Mary gave me confidence as a man that I could indeed be the husband He wanted for her. What's more, it gave her that confidence as well. "I don't always trust you," she said, "but I trust your relationship with God. I know whatever happens between us, you'll go to Him and work things out together."

This growing faith allayed my old fears of both hurting and being hurt in a relationship. In fact, I saw that the freedom I longed for lay not in trusting Mary, but in trusting my Father.

What's more, I no longer needed to fear that in knowing her I would see something negative about her that would have terrible consequences for me. I could accept that she was an imperfect human being like me and that we would both therefore hurt each other from time to time. If I genuinely trusted the Father, I didn't need to envision her as perfect—out of a fear that her imperfections might arise and hurt me. We could work out whatever came up between us if together we cried out to Him.

Indeed, I could ask the Father for courage to face squarely each challenge to us and for wisdom to grow through it together, confident He would stand by me. In fact, I could tell my Father what I wanted. I could pray, "The more I know Mary, the more I love her and want her for my wife. Please, open my heart and make me able to receive all that you have for us together. Teach me to love her as you do."

That's what He was waiting for—not a religious slave, fearful of disobeying Master God's orders and suffering shame and punishment, but a son, trusting the Father to honor my heart and bless my relationship with Mary.

With this foundation, He began to offer supernatural as well as natural confirmation of His calling us together.

Shortly after we set the wedding date, my prayer partner had a strange but compelling vision. "I see you and Mary standing together with her in her wedding gown," he said, "but you're just in your underwear."

Puzzled, we prayed further. "I see you now in a dress shirt," he reported, "but that's all."

Needless to say, at first this was upsetting, as it seemed clearly to confirm my fear that I wasn't ready to get married.

HOLY BRINKSMANSHIP

Eventually, however, I saw that the Father was forcing me into a holy crunch-time brinksmanship. This "count-down trust zone" allowed me only two choices: either to run away and lose the great blessing He had planned for me, or yield my fears to a deeper trust in Him and persevere in the battle to gain it.

It was time for me to step up and fight for what I wanted, even for Mary.

Humbly but fiercely, I cried out to Father God to make me ready. Surrendering to Him time and again, I begged Him to "search my heart" and surface further sins, wounds, or any obstacles to my receiving the gift he was offering me in Mary. I sought healing and deliverance, support and prayer from friends. I read and memorized Scriptures, kept a journal, fasted, continued in counseling, worked out physically, ate healthy, prayed, prayed, and prayed some more.

And when I could do no more, I gave up—not to my fears, but to my Father. "I can't do this, Father," I would simply say, exhaling deeply. "You've got to fight for me here." While I knew I needed to cooperate with His healing process, often that simple prayer of surrender and trust brought me the most peace.

Meanwhile, as the wedding drew closer, each time my friend prayed he saw me more completely dressed. "This time, I see you wearing a black tie," he said one day, and the next time, "Now you've got your vest on."

I confess that this lack of forthright, clear-cut confirmation from Father God continued to frustrate me—even as it drove me deeper into His arms. Self-centered occult divination fuels slavery, stirring fear by focusing simply on the unknown future and unverifiable prediction. In the process of surrendering to God, on the other hand, I was learning to be a son, that is, to engage my Father in the moment, trust His character, and thereby, His purposes in the future.

That's how my dad taught me to swim. First, he held my outstretched hands as I learned to kick, to communicate that he was there for me. Then he let go and stepped back a pace. He remained close enough to catch me if I sank, but far enough to challenge me to paddle toward him—which I did furiously, of course! At first, his letting go felt like abandoning me. But as he kept stepping back, I kept learning to paddle harder to reach him. And before long, I had learned to trust my father's saving hand—and my own ability to swim!

SUPERNATURAL WORD

Two months before the wedding, my friend prayed and saw me standing in my tuxedo trousers. Shortly after that, the Father gave me the supernatural word I'd hoped for, from a trusted prophetic intercessor who wrote me:

> "God has given you a new life, clean slate, fresh start, a new beginning.
>
> He will see you through whatever fears now and in the future. He is with you. He has called you to be in this relationship.
>
> "Trust me to take care of all things. Trust me, Gordon. I have brought you this far; I'm not going to let you fall. I love you, my son. I'm not going to let the past destroy you.
>
> "Fear not, for I am with you. You are precious in my sight and I will be right with you. You know I am here, lean on me. Be not afraid.

Haven't I taken care of you thus far? Won't I do
this now and in the future? I am in complete
control, Gordon. I lead you where you need to
go. I heal you, I love you, I protect you. Do not
be afraid. I am your God and nothing can touch
you when I am with you and I will always be
with you. I am your God.

"Love, God—your Abba Father."

Before that point, my faith had grown to where I didn't really
need this word as a revelation, but I received it gratefully as my Father's
confirmation. It had been a fearful lesson, but I knew that He withheld
that reassurance at first in order to teach me faith in Him, that is, "to be
sure of the things we hope for and to be certain of the things we do not
see" (Heb. 11:1).

On our wedding eve, I was rewarded when my friend saw a vision
of me at the altar, standing resplendent in my tuxedo, from necktie to
shiny shoes.

Again, by then I knew I was ready and was excited to be marrying
Mary. Like any honest groom, however, I had my jitters—and was again
grateful for my Father's encouragement.

Father God had confirmed His desire for Mary and me to marry.
It's not that I married Mary because God told me to, but rather, that I
wanted to marry her and He enabled me to. I'm forever grateful to Him
for it. That's the difference between religion and relationship, both with
God and with each other.

WHO DOES IT

I was ready for marriage, that is, not because I knew how to do it,
but because I knew at last Who does it. I could accept that Mary and
I would at times disappoint and hurt each other. But I had confidence
in my Father for our future. "Everyone has sinned and is far away from
God's saving presence," as Paul declared, "but by the free gift of God's
grace all are put right with him through Christ Jesus, who sets them free"
(Rom. 3:23,24).

Even as myself, the Father had also drawn Mary out of her comfort
zone and into His arms. In fact, Mary's customary dependence upon facts

and natural evidence was pre-empted virtually the moment she first saw me. The pastor of her church, where she was director of the counseling center, had contacted me about my book *Healing the Masculine Soul.* In the course of our conversation, I asked if he knew any women in his congregation who might fit me. Immediately, he told me about Mary.

Later, I was invited to speak there on "Sexuality since Adam and Eve" at a Saturday morning church event. Mary brought her counseling staff and clients to hear me. When I read the scripture, "I will make a suitable companion to help him," she was startled to hear the Father say to her, *And this is your suitable companion.*

Mary had read my book previously when the pastor recommended it to the staff. Knowing nothing about me for her security beyond liking the book, she was upended by God's supernatural word and surrendered it all with a fleece (see Judges 6:36-40). "If that was you speaking, Lord," she prayed, "make him come after me."

During the mid-morning conference break, the pastor and I were chatting together when Mary walked by. He interrupted our conversation to call Mary over, and introduced us briefly. She and I talked about five minutes. I liked her immediately, asked for her business card, and called her shortly afterward. That's how we met.

Later, when the "natural evidence" of our suitability wavered, Mary learned to rely for encouragement upon the Father's supernatural reassurance to her—albeit as uncharacteristic for her as for me to rely on the natural evidence I saw in Mary.

By the time we married, some fears remained, but I felt anchored on the victory side. I had stopped driving myself to measure up and begun instead to trust what the Father was doing in my heart. I had learned to talk over problems and fears with Him—and with Mary when appropriate.

I had stopped pressuring myself to "marry her no matter what" in order to fulfill my engagement commitment, and simply enjoyed being with Mary. I had learned to evaluate our relationship by natural evidence as well as by supernatural revelation, to deal more openly with conflict together, and to grow in confidence as our life values and goals were revealed to be in sync.

Each of us had been badly wounded in previous relationships and developed our own defenses in order to maintain control. In His fierce grace, God had summarily removed those defenses and forced us to trust

His control. Together—both naturally and supernaturally—we were learning not how to make our marriage work, but how to let God work in our marriage.

It was harder and more fearful work than I'd ever known, then or since. It was a pitched battle, fought in the spirit realm and in my heart.

Through it all, however, Mary and I gained a far deeper faith in the Father, and thereby, a confidence in His purposes for us—which has allowed us increasingly to trust and enjoy each other over the years. At times, like all growing couples, we have our conflicts. But we've never forgotten God's promise in that season years ago, "I will restore to you the years which the swarming locusts have eaten" (Joel 2:25).

Pure Sex

Small-Group Interaction

Questions

FOREWORD

1. Why does the idea of sexuality and spirituality together sound unusual?

2. "Church is the last place you expect to hear someone talking about sex."

Why do you think that's true? What does this say about church?

3. "Certainly, He'll find religion aplenty, that is, people striving to prove they're good—or at least, better than you—without ever confessing they can't be good and crying out for a savior." (p.10) What's the author's problem with religion? Have you ever seen what he describes about it in this sentence? Have you ever felt that aspect of religion in yourself?

4. "Workers protest for minimum wage, while a woman gets paid thousands of dollars for simply taking off her clothes in front of a camera." Why is that true? What does this say about our culture and how we think about sexuality?

INTRODUCTION

1. "Sexual desire is a spiritual phenomenon." (p. 16) What makes the author think that? Do you agree? Why or why not?

2. The author says that he went to church all his life growing up, but "I had never been so seized by a Sunday School lesson or sermon" as by what happened on the school bus. Why not? Why was the "lesson" taught by the older kid so impacting?

3. After the school bus incident, why didn't the boy go to his father and ask his Dad about sex? Did your parent(s) ever have "The Talk" with you when you began growing up? If you're a parent with older children, did you talk to them about it when they began growing up? If so, was it difficult? Why or why not? What advice would you offer other parents about that, from your own experience?

CHAPTER 1

1. Why is the father so significant to a child's sense of gender identity—both for the boy and for the girl?

2. The author says he's challenged Christian women around the world to come together and design a program to teach a dad what his daughter needs from him. Why do you think so few women have done that? What would it take for your church to do it?

3. What does "sexual overload" mean? How do you think it affects young people today? What choices does the world offer to deal with it? What could your church do to help young people deal with it?

4. "The God who created desire has come in Jesus to promote authentic sexual freedom." (p.29) What do you think "sexual freedom" means to God?

CHAPTER 2

1. In what sense does the author say that sexual desire is a "holy nostalgia"? Do you agree? Why or why not?

2. What does the author say is the difference between being alone and being lonely? (p. 37) Does that ring true to your own experience?

3. How is the mother's womb like the Garden of Eden?

4. "If the man has not broken the emotional tie to his mother, his sexual desire for his wife will be hijacked by his boyhood longing for

Mom." (p.41) What do you think this means? Do you agree? Why or why not?

5. The author confesses that, as a man, "I cannot speak for women" about this desire to go back to the mother's womb. How do you think this dynamic works for women? Or doesn't it? What difference does it mean for sexual attraction in women and in men?

CHAPTER 3

1. What does the term "suitable companion" mean to you about choosing a mate?

2. Why is a sense of calling or purpose in life important to marriage partners?

3. How did the author misunderstand God's word to him as a single man, "Pray for the woman"? Certainly, it's easy to believe God could also tell a young woman, "Pray for the man." How does praying like that help a single Christian who wants to be married?

4. What does the Apostle Paul say are the benefits of being single? (p.56) What encouragement would you give to a single man or woman who's looking for a marriage partner?

CHAPTER 4

1. What does "Naked but not Ashamed" mean apart from physical nakedness? Why is that an uncomfortable place to be?

2. What part of the author's dramatic take on Adam's story impacts you most? Why? What other significant aspect of that story do you see that's not in the book?

3. "Therefore...the two shall become one flesh." Why? What does the Bible imply here is the root of sexual attraction?

CHAPTER 5

1. What is it that's "flawed, broken, or defective in our human nature" that "stirs shame and is related to sexuality"? (p.76)

2. Is modesty just about religious guilt or cultural taboo? If not, where do you think the impulse to "be modest" comes from?

3. "Today's widespread sexual exposure, urged by popular media,… comes at a severe cost, especially to women." (p.78) Why does the media promote it? What is that cost to women? What would make a woman willing to pay it? How might Christians overcome this influence by the media?

CHAPTER 6

1. Until recently, before female doctors, a woman had no choice for a gynecologist besides a male doctor. What made the author wonder how that affects a woman? How does it affect a woman? (Can any woman in the group explain this to the men?)

2. The author says that in previous generations, men were not so concerned about modesty as they are today. Do you agree? If so, why do you think that's true?

CHAPTER 7

1. As a pastor, the author felt the women in his mostly single congregation were not dressing appropriately for church. Have you ever felt that way at your church? What were the author's first thoughts about how to handle that problem? How do you feel about the way he finally decided to handle it?

2. Until a woman pointed it out to him, the author was not aware that the men in the congregation were also not dressing appropriately. Do you think the women's viewpoint on this are less likely to be heard? What else about a woman's experience of church does not get expressed when all the leaders are men?

CHAPTER 8

1. How does the author say things have changed in public schools since his youth regarding the way students dress? Have you seen changes

since your high school days in this regard? If so, would you say for the better or for the worse? If worse, what do you think can be done about it?

2. The author implies that often parents of teenage girls don't know how to talk to their daughters about how they dress. What do you think about his advice to moms and dads? What would you add to or subtract from that?

3. "Femininity blossoms amid security....masculinity thrives amid the challenge of insecurity." (p.99) Do you agree with this or not? Why or why not?

CHAPTER 9

1. "How could someone so gifted in ministry fall so hard to temptation?" (p.101) How would you answer that question? When a particular mega church pastor fell, what was the author's problem with the "righteous outrage" from other Christian leaders?

2. What power does religious law have to save us from falling? What power does it lack? In what sense does a legal command itself stir sin?

3. Why does God set sexual boundaries? How does the notion of "sexual needs" sabotage those boundaries?

4. "Jesus cried out in pain and wept in sorrow as he offered up priestly prayers to God." (p.108) Have you ever prayed that deeply? How would you say God answered your prayer?

5. "The rules and punishment of religion may identify the sin, but can't stop the urge to sin nor save you from its effects." (p.110) So what can we do when religion doesn't work?

CHAPTER 10

1. Why did memories of past sexual experiences come to Barry's mind when he was with Sally?

2. Why doesn't God want His children to have sex before marriage?

3. What are the "spiritual consequences of sexual union"? Why don't most Christians know this? How has God provided to overcome those consequences?

4. Would anyone in the group like to testify to that?

CHAPTER 11

1. How does the author say that the Church has shaped our ideas about sexuality?

2. What does she mean by actions which "objectify women"? How have you (women) seen or experienced this yourself? Are any men in the group aware of this?

3. "For a woman, sexual intercourse is only one ingredient that contributes to true intimacy." (p. 132) What does the author suggest are some other ingredients?

4. Why does the marriage covenant make sex better for a woman?

5. In what sense do "women tend to lose power when they initiate sex quickly in a relationship"? (p. 134) Why might a woman do that? How do you think Father God feels about that?

CHAPTER 12

1. What harm does pedophilia cause in the child victim? Why is Jesus so deeply concerned about that?

2. In what sense does Jesus identify with a child? Why is it hard for most of us adults to do so?

3. What spiritual dynamic motivates an adult to become a pedophile? How has Jesus provided to overcome that?

CHAPTER 13

1. Why did the Christian groom ask for "Tasteful gifts only" at his bachelor party?

2. Why were the Christian men at the party unsure what else to do there? Why do you think the men responded so enthusiastically to the author's suggestion?

3. What additional suggestions would you offer for a Christian bachelor party?

CHAPTER 14

1. What does the author suggest is the basic root of homosexual feelings? How does he say historical events have led to sexual confusion among men today? Would you agree? Why or why not?

2. How could a man-hating spirit take root in a man, and how might that affect his sexuality?

3. How did Father God lead the author to discover and cast out the man-hating spirit from himself? How did that free him as a man?

4. Why do you think such a viewpoint might not be accepted today?

CHAPTER 15

1. Why is religion threatened by sexual attraction to the point of largely not acknowledging it?

2. Why do we often consider only certain sexual acts as "immoral" rather than other harmful behaviors?

3. "Grace is different from the law in that the favor comes before the obedience." (p.175) Why do you think God would give us favor before we obey Him? Why is it so hard for human beings—and so many Christians--to understand this grace? Why do you think that in the world favor comes after obedience? How have you experienced a) the way of the world and b) the way of grace in your own life?

4. Why is grace so important to sexual expression in a marriage?

CHAPTER 16

1. How did the spirit of religion show itself in the author's fears about getting married?

2. When the pastor told his congregation that he married his wife because God told him to, why did the women groan?

3. "Disconnected from my heart, lacking confidence in my emotional responses, I had nothing to gauge my responses beyond what I should feel and should do." (p.189) Have you ever felt this way yourself? How did that affect you? What does it take to reconnect to your heart? Give an example from your own life.

4. Why did God not give the author a clear and direct word about marrying Mary until he had come to a decision on his own?

5. Why did God confirm His word for them each in a way directly opposite from their usual gifting?

6. What have you gained by reading this book and sharing with the others in your group?

About the Authors

Gordon Dalbey's widely acclaimed classic *Healing the Masculine Soul* helped pioneer the men's movement in 1988 and remains a bestseller today, with French and Italian translations. A popular speaker at conferences and retreats around the US and world, he has ministered in England, Hong Kong, Australia, New Zealand, Italy, France, Switzerland, Canada, and South Africa. A former news reporter (Charlotte NC), Peace Corps Volunteer (Nigeria), high school teacher (Chicago, San Jose CA) and pastor (Los Angeles), he holds an M.Div. from Harvard Divinity School, an M.A. in journalism from Stanford, and a B.A. from Duke.

The author of eight books, Gordon has appeared on *Focus on the Family* and many other radio and TV programs. His magazine publications include *Reader's Digest, The Los Angeles Times, Catholic Digest, Leadership Journal, Christian Century*, and *New Man*. He lives in Santa Barbara, CA, and may be reached at www.abbafather.com.

Mary Andrews-Dalbey holds a doctorate in professional psychology and a master's degree in nursing. She has been a pediatric and psychiatric nurse, Christian counselor, and director of a ministry to pregnant, unwed women. She now counsels families at a child-abuse prevention agency. Mary has spoken internationally at women's conferences. Her book *The REST of Your Life, Discovering God's Rest in a Driven, Demanding, Distressful World* portrays how true rest is not about what we don't do, but about what God does. Her psychological and medical and backgrounds, along with her ministry leadership experience, have given her a unique approach to healing from a spiritual, emotional, and physical perspective.

Other Gordon Dalbey books
Paperbacks/audio cd/mp3 at
www.abbafather.com
ebooks at www.kindle.com

Both refreshing and upending, Gordon Dalbey's books for men take us to depths of authentic manhood where we're humbled by its mystery and engaged by its call. Apart from either violence or lust, these books restore both courage and passion to manhood. Here's a masculinity you can trust—and the Father who makes it happen.

Healing the Masculine Soul

Today, politically correct voices cry out for men to be more sensitive, to tame our masculine nature. Meanwhile, the media bombards us with "macho" images of violence and lust. Is it any wonder men today are left bewildered about what manhood really is?

This pioneering, bestselling classic gives men hope for restoration by showing how Jesus enables us to get real with ourselves, with Him, and with other men. Its refreshing journey into the masculine soul dares men to break free from deceptive stereotypes and discover the power and blessing of authentic manhood.

Sons of the Father
Healing the Father-Wound in Men Today

"When you became a dad for the first time, did your own dad reach out to you with support, encouragement, or helpful advice?" Out of 350 Christian fathers, only 5 hands went up. "When you were 11 or 12, did your father talk to you about sex and relating to women?" I asked another gathering of 150 Christian men. Two hands.

Men today suffer a deep father-wound, which has left us unequipped for manhood. The father of Lies capitalizes on its shame and blackmails us into isolation, denial, and a host of bogus cover-ups—from money and guns to alcohol, sex, and performance religion.

The true Father of all men has come in Jesus to draw us back to Himself and to the man He created you to be. Here's the map to get you there.

Fight like a Man:
A New Manhood for a New Warfare

9/11 revealed the enemy of God and humanity as rooted in shame-based religion. The focus of warfare has now shifted dramatically from military battles to the hearts of men.

Fight like a Man focuses on the crippling byproduct of fatherlessness in men today, namely, shame—too often fostered by religion, always overcome by Jesus. It's not about how to be a man, but knowing the Father who rescues and restores men. It's not even about how to be a warrior, but surrendering to the Commander of the Lord's Army.

Here, you won't be exhorted to obey, but invited to trust. You won't be commanded to do it right, but freed to be real. You won't be warned to be strong, but promised your Father's strength as you experience the grace and dignity of being His son.

> Gordon Dalbey's books will stir you to a faith both passionate about its truth and compassionate in its grace. Here's freedom from universal tolerance on the one hand and narrow condemnation on the other—and Jesus at work today as God's vital Third Option to the world's self-defeating enmity.

Do Pirates Wear Pajamas?
And Other Mysteries in the Adventure of Fathering

"Daddy, it's not an adventure unless it's a little scary!"

The lessons of fathering are the character of God.

Watch for what God is doing in your child, and bless it.

In these impacting, real-life stories, you'll meet a bestselling Christian author who's a dad in on-the-job training—sometimes stumbling, sometimes celebrating, always learning. Experience teaches us the best lessons. But too often, we men miss the experience because we fear the shame of not knowing how to do it.

There's good news here for us dads: We're in this adventure together as men, and the Father of us all stands with us. You don't have to know how to do it. You just need to know Who does it—and trust Him to give you what you need to be the dad your child needs.

No Small Snakes
A Journey into Spiritual Warfare

This is my upending personal story of meeting and learning to overcome the powers of evil as portrayed in the Bible.

The problem in confronting spiritual reality, I discovered, is not that our childish imagination gets hooked into foolish fears, but that something real is evil and we can't control it. This humbling truth stirs shame in our Western, control-oriented culture and we deny the reality of supernatural evil. But pretending there's no thief in your house doesn't protect you from being robbed; it only gives thieves free rein to steal whatever they want.

In Jesus, God has invited us to exchange the illusion of our control for the reality of His power. This book extends that invitation to you.

> **The awful wounding of our times, from family breakups and sexual confusion to drugs and violence, has left us hungry for a faith that embraces reality as graphically as we're forced to in this increasingly lost and broken world.**

Broken by Religion, Healed by God
Restoring the Evangelical, Sacramental, Pentecostal, Social Justice Church

This is my story of how I became born again among Evangelicals, discovered the sacrament among Catholics, received the baptism of the Spirit among Pentecostals, and was awakened to social justice ministries among Oldline Reformers. But it's also about the crippling brokenness in the Body of Christ today, which that journey revealed—how the Church has divided itself by these four very ways people meet Jesus, sabotaging its credibility and mission.

The same spirits of shame and division which animated the Pharisees and 9/11 terrorists have for centuries distracted Christians from what Jesus is doing and kept us from seeing each other as He does. Here's how to join Jesus as He battles unto today to heal His broken Body—and through it, this broken world.

Religion vs Reality
Facing the Home Front in Spiritual Warfare

Go figure out what this scripture means: "I'm after mercy, not religion. I'm here to invite outsiders, not to coddle insiders." (Matt. 9:13,14TMB)

Since Jesus, religion is obsolete.

Religion is our human effort to cover the shame of our sin-nature. Honest human beings know it doesn't work. In fact, that's why Jesus came—not to cover our shame but to remove it. He thereby revealed religion as a tool of the enemy to distract us from His work.

The power of evil unmasks this false security of religion. And so our sophisticated Western pride denies the reality of evil because it reminds us we're not in control. Tragically, we thereby forfeit the power to overcome it. Here's how to reclaim that power.

Chapters focus on works of the enemy often hidden by popular culture and religious denial. Titles include Facing Spiritual Denial, 9/11 and the Spirit of Religion, Ball Games and the Battle for Men's Souls, Homosexualityand the Father Wound, White Racism and Spiritual Imperialism, Unmasking Halloween, Overcoming Depression, and Delivered from Abortion.

Loving to Fight, or Fighting to Love?
Winning the Spiritual Battle for Your Marriage
with Mary Andrews-Dalbey, PhD

"God created man in his own image,…male and female he created them" (Gen. 1:27)

Our spiritual enemy's most deliberate efforts to distort the image of God focus on His most fundamental reflection in this world—namely, on the union of "male and female." Amid this widespread attack on marriages, the divorce rate among Christians is the same as among others at about 33%. Clearly, the overcoming power God has given to His church is not being widely received and exercised by Christian couples.

"They say marriages are made in heaven," actor Clint Eastwood once commented. "So are thunder and lightning." In this fallen world, storms come to every honest couple. Those who fight in the power of the flesh think the question is, Who's right? But for those who fight in the power of the Spirit, the question is, What's God trying to teach us?

This book is therefore not about how to make your marriage work, but how to let God work in your marriage. Chapters include Never Waste a Good Fight, Leaving Father and Mother: The Trailhead to Marriage, For Better or Worse: A Woman's View (Mary), When You're Hot You're Hot; When You're not It's Time to Talk about Sex, and A Couples' Guide to Spiritual Warfare.

The REST of Your Life
Finding God's Rest in a Driven, Demanding, Distressful World

By Mary Andrews-Dalbey, PhD

We're tired. We're stressed. We're over-extended. But we can't stop. Too often, we stay busy in order to make ourselves acceptable and cover up a sense of shame and inadequacy. At the end of creation, God rested—not because He was tired, but because He was finished. Likewise, we can surrender to His finished work on the cross and enter His Sabbath Rest. The rest God offers does not require the luxury of a settled life, but rather, the comfort of a secured soul that trusts and relies on Him. The Sabbath, therefore, is not about what you don't do, but about what God does. Even in the midst of our daily responsibilities, we can find security and serenity as He's working in our lives.

NOTES

1   "Diana Oh Is Wearing Lingerie in Public to Reclaim Women's
    Sexuality," *Huffpost Women*, 11/21/14   http://www.huffingtonpost.
    com/2014/11/18/diana-oh-my-lingerie-play_n_6178188.
    html?icid=maing-grid7%7Chtmlws-main-bb%7Cdl12%7Csec1_
    lnk3%26pLid%3D568321
2   Shikha Dalmia, *Reason* magazine, quoted in Matt Pearce, " 'Yes means yes'
    divides liberals," *Los Angeles Times*, 10/27/14, AA2.
3   Wendy Shalit, *A Return to Modesty* (New York: Free Press, 1999).
4   *Los Angeles Times* 5/8/14 p. A17.
5   Donna Musil, *BRATS: Our Journey Home* (Eatonton, GA: Brats Without
    Borders, Inc., 2005)www.bratsourjourneyhome.com.
6   Sony/ATV Songs LLC, 1968.
7   https://www.goodreads.com/author/quotes/7921.Thomas_Wolfe
8   Herb Nacio Brown and Gordon Clifford, 1932
9   A Jim Beam ad. I have the *Newsweek* page cutout, but neglected to note
    the date.
10 *The American Heritage College Dictionary* (Boston: Houghton Mifflin,
    2004), 1127.
11 http://canadanouvelles.net/item/19101_ex-model-62-nearly-bares-all-in-
    interview
12 published in *Leadership*, summer 2001, 56-57.
13 Clarence Tucker Craig, "Introduction to 1 Corinthians," *Interpreter's Bible*
    (New York: Abingdon, 1952), Vol. X, 34.
14 John and Paula Sandford, *The Transformation of the Inner Man* (S.
    Plainfield, NJ: Bridge Publishing Company, 1982), 277-278.
15 Kinsey, A.; W. Pomeroy; C. Martin, & P. Gebhard: *Sexual Behavior in the
    Human Female* (Philadelphia: Saunders, 1953).
16 Wikipedia, *The Free Encyclopedia*, "Kinsey Reports, Main Findings."
17 *Ibid.*
18 *American Heritage College Dictionary* (Boston: Houghton Mifflin, 2004),
    1132.
19 Stevens, Evelyn P.: "Marianismo: The Other Face of Machismo in Latin
    America" in Pescatelo, Ann, *Female and Male in Latin America* (Pittsburgh:
    University of Pittsburgh Press, 1973).
20 Villegas, Jorge; Jennifer Lemanski, & Carlos Valdéz. "Marianismo And
    Machismo: The Portrayal Of Females In Mexican TV Commercials."
    Journal Of International Consumer Marketing 22.4 (2010): 327-346.
21 Field, Samanta: "How Purity Culture and Raunch Culture Objectify
    Women," posted on June 12, 2014. http://www.convergentbooks.com/
    how-purity-culture-and-raunch-culture-objectify-women/